FUL
AMEF

MW01173599

Chapters:

FULFILLING MY AMERCIAN DREAM!

CHAPTER ONE

The Empire of Gold

(Gállány Cosmetic)

1. <u>Who is Ida today? (2018)</u>

The launch of her new product line was everything Ida Gal-Csiszar had imagined! *The Essential Palette* had been featured in fashion magazines *Harper's Bazaar*, *Vanity*, and *Elle* and in June, 2017 it was simultaneously introduced at a posh event at the exclusive hotel in Hollywood and on QVC, America's biggest home shopping network broadcasting to 350 million households in seven countries!

The party at The London which was held in the Vivienne Penthouse with a 360 degree rooftop view, attracted celebrities who wore Ida's makeup in colors such as *Vogue'd*, *Cashmere*, *Iris*, *Vintage*, *Velvet*, and *Milk & Honey*.

FULFILLING MY AMERCIAN DREAM!

Some may not have heard of Ida Gal-Csiszar, but her products have made it onto the big screen, the small screen, and to make-up counters everywhere. Ida is a Hungarian-American, award-winning beauty industry mogul who teamed up with Hollywood celebrity makeup artist, Billy B., to curate *The Essential Palette*. As one of the most successful and sought-after experts in the entertainment industry, his client list includes: Lady Gaga, Cindy Crawford, Charlize Theron, Sharon Stone, Beyoncé, Sandra Bullock, Jennifer Lopez, Pink, Britney Spears, and Mary J. Blige. When the opportunity rose to collaborate with Ida, Billy B. immediately jumped on it because "she understands the textures and formulas that I would feel confident putting my name on."

Her stylish signature product, *The Essential Palette*, is presented in an elegant, antique gold box consisting of 19 eye and face colors. They were all constructed in the laboratory of Ida's own California cosmetic manufacturing facility, Classic Cosmetics, that employs 350 people.

FULFILLING MY AMERCIAN DREAM!

The extravagant design of the space at The London reflected the hues of *The Essential Palette* and transformed the fête into a vivacious and hip haven. Guests were greeted with summer cocktails as they walked through the entrance witnessing walls lined with pink cotton candy wrapped in orange reflective cellophane adorned with cheerful bows. The panels of tangerine, purple, and red roses reached all the way up to the ceiling and Ida—a vibrant 80-year old icon—appeared with her signature bright red lipstick.

What led to all this professional success was Ida's creation of her very own makeup line, *Gállány*, just a few years before. Currently, the brand consists of close to 100 items of various shades of lipsticks, lip glosses, eye shadows, blushes, concealers, foundations, and mascara, available for purchase on the world wide web.

Before Ida launched her cosmetic line and become an idol whose presence was requested at Academy Awards ceremonies, she was the master make-up chemist behind many of the most famous American beauty industry products that you see on the shelves today. She was also a lead liquid chemist and "a pillar of the factory" at the color laboratory for Max Factor, Hollywood's pioneer makeup company. Prior to that, she was a quality control manager at the headquarters of the multinational Fortune 500 Company, Johnson & Johnson, specializing in medical devices, pharmaceutical, and consumer packaged goods.

Being on top of the makeup industry is fascinating but her inspiring "rags to riches" journey full of trials and tribulations a hundred times more so!

CHAPTER TWO

The Farm of True Poppy Coral

(Hungary: 1939 – November, 1956)

2. Hungary: 1939 – November, 1956

Ida Gal was born in 1939—the year World War II broke out—into a loving, devoted, large, and well-to-do family in a small, agricultural, and idyllic village of Gyoma (currently Gyomaendrőd) in Hungary, about 20 miles west of the Romanian border.

Her father, Ferenc, was a farmer and her mother, Vilma, a homemaker. Her parents had five children; Ida was their second. Her siblings were Irene (b. 1937), Lenke (b. 1944), Ferenc (b. 1946), and Istvan (b. 1949). Her caring and tight-knit family gave Ida a strong emotional foundation and her great-aunt, who previously spent years in the United States, gave her inspiration and an undying thirst for life.

FULFILLING MY AMERCIAN DREAM!

Ida's hardworking, middle-class family spent most of their time on their spacious 15-acre farm—the largest in the area—that provided them with the "most beautiful life you could ask for." The property was about four miles from the county seat and consisted of farm houses, a root cellar, an orchard, a vineyard, a stable, a chicken coop, a grassy area, and a deep well with a counterweight pole. There were two dirt roads, one of them led directly to their house, which happened to be the last property in town and close to a local castle. They focused on growing corn, caring for their cows and chickens with the help of several farm workers and a resident hayward. They owned four horses and, raised racehorses as well. As a little girl, Ida regularly heard the sound of the foals galloping towards their farm—a comforting and soothing sound of the country. In addition, Ida's father, who was a highly skilled individual, was in demand to assist on other local ranches. He primarily helped relatives to work the land in exchange for financial payment or produce.

FULFILLING MY AMERCIAN DREAM!

While the Gals had another home in the center of the town, they preferred to stay on their simple and sizable farm which had no electricity. Her mother had four sisters and a brother. Her father had seven siblings, so Ida grew up with plenty of cousins to play with when they visited. Her parents were one hundred percent devoted to the happiness of their children and gave them everything they could afford.

The best time of her life was on the ranch in the summers. She played all day and sometimes all night, swam in the river, and rode her bicycle everywhere. Extended family members from various cities would join them when the kids were off from school and their bunch was allowed to roam freely. June, July, and August meant paradise for the youngsters and adults alike. They played hide-and-seek along with other amusing games. It was noisy and happy; everybody was cooking or baking and having tons of fun. They had fresh food in their own backyard: tasty chickens, big eggs, delicious fruit, firm green beans, lush berries, and so much more.

FULFILLING MY AMERCIAN DREAM!

Ida was "a daddy's girl." She adored her soft-spoken father who never yelled or raised his voice. Ferenc was a caring and gentle man who lost his father at an early age, whereas Ida's mother had a different personality. While Vilma adored her children, she was quick-tempered and whenever she got angry, she would not hesitate to scream or even grab them by the hair.

Even though Ida's parents believed in God, they were not particularly religious. Ida's paternal grandfather passed away when he was young. The rest of her grandparents, especially her maternal grandfather, were deeply religious and attended services regularly. Her grandpa's faith was so strong that he often made the family go to services with him. Instead of protesting it, the Gals obediently carried on the customs and culture of Protestantism. They baptized all their children when they were born and celebrated all the Christian holidays including Christmas and Easter. Ida was not a big believer in God; as a matter of fact, religion left very little imprint on her as a youngster. She certainly didn't believe in miracles or divine Providence; although once in a while it occurred to her that perhaps she was, in fact, being guided by a mystical power.

Ida was a well-behaved but peculiar and philosophical child. She was a loner and an introvert but a happy one, at least until the Communists invaded the region. She didn't like people around because, she felt, others interrupted her solitude and musing. She entertained herself by daydreaming while doing chores. As a child she wanted to play on her own but because she had four siblings, she couldn't just push them away. She saw beauty and art in everything and was fascinated with color and textures. She was sensory-oriented, and her love for and physical closeness to trees, flowers, bushes, and the earth were important to her. She adored gardening and growing luscious plants in the soil.

Ida hated school but not because of the subjects they taught but rather she didn't like being bossed around all the time. In the 50s, teachers had a very different way of conducting the classes. They were harsh, aggressive, pedantic, meticulous, and sometimes used corporal punishment; today it would be considered child abuse. The so called Prussian educational style was not Ida's cup of tea. Instead, she wanted to be in control and self-ruling. While she always took care of what needed to be handled, such as her homework and chores around the house, she preferred to do them on her own terms. She was self-motivated and did things well the first time around which governed her excelling later in life. Self-admittedly she always gave her 110%. She had an aversion to being pushed or instructed what to do. As a first grader she was interested in everything and had a lot of curiosity; she was especially fascinated by biographies. She was full of energy and as she grew, she wanted to continuously expand and explore.

No matter how perfect her life seemed, Ida somehow felt out of place and, therefore, had a compulsive urge to find something in her life. What that something was, she didn't know so she started to listen to her instinct more and more. Even though she was still a minor, she was constantly wondering about life and trying to figure out why she was born in such a small town. Why was last name Gal? Why did her grandparents end up in that region? And why did she grow up on that particular farm?

In 1941, Hungary entered World War II which wasn't good news for Ida's family. In March 1944, Germany invaded their homeland. The same year, in November, the first Soviet tank reached the border of Hungary and the country became a battle ground.

Seeking increased safety, the Gals moved to their residence into the heart of Gyoma while the hayward stayed on and watched over their farm. However, once the bombings started, the family realized that their town was just too close to one of the major targets, Bekescsaba. Trying to escape significant injuries from the scattered shrapnel, the family decided to move back to their farmland, a far less populated area and less of a military aim. Even the grandparents moved out to the farm with them. All the Gals wanted to do was to survive the battles without any major loss while Ida's father was forced to do military service on the German side. Despite, no matter how much they attempted to avoid the threats of the era, they could not avoid the inevitable…

On a sunny morning, the family decided to check on the grandparents' house. While the adults were chatting near the building, Ida was playing in the sandbox in the garden under her nana's favorite lilac tree. Suddenly, a fast and loud airplane—named Gigant—appeared. Ida's family had seen this type of jet before; the aircraft was always flying low because—they were told—it was transporting tanks and cross-continental trucks. This time it seemed to be so very close to the ground that it appeared to touch the top of the tree under which Ida was standing. It all happened instantly and there was no time for her relatives to get to the four-year old girl who got so petrified standing there all alone and helpless, she wet herself. This was one of Ida's first humiliating memories of the war that left her deeply traumatized.

Unfortunately, this was not the only time Ida had to go through a near death experience. One day, as bomber airplanes were approaching their farm house, Vilma alarmed grabbed Ida, Irene, and baby Lenke in the stroller, and tried to rush over to the neighbor's house before the Gal residence was destroyed. However, one of the pilots spotted them running on the ground half way between. It became alarmingly obvious that instead of the buildings, he was now going to go after the frightened family. While Irene was pulling, Vilma and Ida were pushing the highly visible white stroller on the dirt road as fast as they could. Once the pilot started to shoot at them, Vilma took the baby out of the carriage and they all ran into the corn field. Corn is a tall plant, sometimes reaching seven to eight feet high; nonetheless, it was after harvest time and the workers had already cut down the stalks and organized them in heaps, making the four of them still visible. Having no other option, they dove into the largest stack and prayed for their lives…

Once the bombers left, Ida and her family found the stroller riddled with bullet holes. Leaving deep-rooted psychological scars not always visible when you talk to her, the attack had re-surfaced in Ida's dreams over and over again for many years.

While the Soviets were retreating after WW II, they temporarily occupied their land. They adored Lenke who, at the time, was still a darling newborn. Missing their own children, the men frequently grabbed the infant and carried her aroud. Each time they took the baby out Vilma's arms, she was incredibly scared but she had to let them have fun with her, otherwise the family would have risked getting shot.

It was common knowledge that the Hungarian population was frightened of the Russians who were infamous for their extreme barbaric behavior—raping women and confiscating food everywhere they went, since the stationing army was not well supplied. The Gals were fortunate because the officers on their acreage were fairly humane. So much so that when there was a threat by the occupying soldiers at the neighbors' house, they would ask these officers to assist with the problem. They would then pay a visit and instruct those soldiers to knock it off and they did. Unlike most of them, these were not violent, assaulted no one, and seemed to be the more intelligent than the rest of the army members. Given the situation, Ida's family felt lucky to have civilized soldiers occupying their estate, especially because all the Gal women came to their farm during the battles including Ida's aunts, grandmothers, mother, and sisters.

Even Ida's favorite great-aunt was there having moved back to Hungary from America before World War II broke out. Lidia Bogoly was Ida's grandfather's sister. She emigrated to the United States before World War I when she was in her late teens, mostly working as a cook and housekeeper for upscale households in New York and Florida. While Ida's great-aunt was in America, she frequently sent gorgeous gifts to the family. All of Lidia's lavish presents were breathtakingly beautiful, classy, and exquisite; most certainly the rustic environment amplified their uniqueness.

FULFILLING MY
AMERCIAN DREAM!

While overseas, Lidia saved diligently and upon returning to Gyoma, she was able to transfer a lot of money. In addition, she got rather lucky with the conversion rate of the American dollar to the Hungarian Forint. So much so, that she was able to buy a large property in town and build an impressive house on it as well as purchase a smaller dwelling in the city.

Upon relocating, Lidia brought a lot of gorgeous things back with her: furniture, hats, jewelry, dresses, gloves, and many items that seemed more than luxurious, especially in an Eastern European countryside.

When Ida saw all the shiny and upscale things that Lidia purchased, Ida's jaw dropped and all she could say was "My God!". Mind you, Communists don't believe in the existence of God or allow religious practices, so as the regime was later established, just by saying those words, Ida became a little rebel herself.

FULFILLING MY AMERCIAN DREAM!

Lidia was particularly attached to her American bed; she not only shipped the frame home, but the mattress as well. She even let Ida jump on it endlessly, which was tremendous amount of fun, while her strict parents never allowed the same. Ida associated her aunt with freedom and joy; Lidia exuded what Ida imagined America to be. The young lady was endlessly drawn to her aunt's beautiful possessions especially because Ida already was a highly aesthetic person. Her aunt also took her New World ficus tree to Gyoma which Ida adored. Some of the fascinating stories Lidia told her were about fashionable high society balls and American landmarks, things about which Ida hadn't yet heard up to this point. She was captivated by all the intriguing descriptions and the more Ida heard the more longing she developed. She felt America was where she belonged and this feeling gave Ida a lot of determination to go there one day and visit the Empire State Building.

It didn't take long before Lidia became Ida's inspiration. Due to her influence, Ida's sister, Irene, and Ida developed a little girls' game among themselves: they both babbled and dreamt about marrying an American man. Ida definitely wanted to be the wife of a captain and Irene was set on becoming the bride of a pilot.

Meanwhile, Ferenc survived the war and was lucky enough to return home unharmed. Just as he was ready to celebrate the fact that he made it, there was another danger hovering. As the Soviets were retreating from Hungary, they not only took all of the horses the Gals owned but they took many local men as prisoners of war—including Ida's father. They forced them to walk dozens of miles alongside the army which consisted of horses, cars, tanks, and various other vehicles. Once they got close to the Romania border, Ida's father started to look for opportunities to escape. He had managed to withstand the horrors of the war; he was not going to freeze to death in a Siberian labor camp now! So, as they were marching, the army captain suddenly instructed them to take a brief break and had the POWs sit down near a ditch. Once everyone started to move forward again, Ida's father and his buddy hid in the trench unnoticed and waited until the Russians left.

When the coast was clear, they started the walk back home which took quite a while even though the distance was not that great. Afraid of being caught, they halted during day and hiked at night to minimize being noticed. When they spotted a building they approached it cautiously, keeping an eye on it for a day or two to determine whether there were any infantry around. Once they concluded that there weren't, they approached the owner, asked for something to eat, and then continued walking to Gyoma.

When Ferenc finally got close to their ranch, the two horses—that escaped injured from the Soviets and found their way home again—must have recognized him because they started to neigh and scratch the ground. The family heard the noise but, of course, had no idea why. When he went inside, the entire family was overjoyed, but they only saw him briefly. The reason being that while Ida's father was away, it was announced that if anyone saw any prisoners of war who had escaped, the public needed to report them immediately. Though the officials stated that escapees would not be subject to harm, Ferenc practiced caution. The next day he went to the town center and decided to disclose his presence. There he met a previous laborer who used to work for him. Ida's father always treated his employees with respect and with this one, he even had a kinship. During the fighting the man became a Communist and started to work for the administration. Once he saw his former boss, the young leftist told him to "disappear immediately for months until everything settled down" and the Soviets had retreated completely. He suggested for Ferenc "not to be seen anywhere." Meanwhile, his buddy with whom he escaped also announced himself to the authorities. He didn't have any friends in the administration and they never saw him again…

Ida's father went into hiding and the children didn't see him for a long, long time. They thought their father had been taken away again, which confused them, since there was no war anymore.

Vilma's brother, Jozsef Jr., wasn't as lucky as Ferenc. He attended an anti-Communist military academy that later was turned into a Communists institution upon which he was deported to a North

Asian labor camp. The region is known for its harsh climate with long and brutally cold winters. For many, being taken there was equated with a death sentence. Most died or were not allowed to return home, ever. The Gals collectively prayed for Jozsef's survival and unlike most—perhaps due to his disciplined and strict military training—he survived the harsh environment, and after six years, he returned home at the age 24. From that point on he was considered a hero, and all of them looked up to him.

Vilma's father, Jozsef Sr., was closely tied to the military as well. He saved a fellow soldier's life in a fire and for his courage he was granted a status of valor. Ida still proudly displays his certificate on her office wall. Due to recent changes of the regulations, women now too can inherit their relatives' valor status and if Ida requested it, she could become one. All the same, she has never been interested in such standing but takes a glance at the proof of her grandfather's bravery every day.

The Invasion of Classic Red

(Communism)

Communism, which Ida hated so much, came to power in a very particular way in Hungary. It all started during World War II when the Soviet Army occupied the country in September 1944. The siege of Budapest lasted almost two months and it was the longest successful siege of any city in the entire war. The city suffered widespread destruction and all of the bridges over the Danube in the capital were blown up by the Germans in an effort to slow down the Soviet advance.

In 1947, Hungary signed the Peace Treaty of Paris and many of the Communist leaders of 1919, who emigrated to the Soviet Union at the time, returned to Hungary. The Soviets originally planned for a piecemeal introduction of the regime. Due to the demands of the Western Allies for a democratic election, the Soviets authorized the only essentially free-election held in post-war Eastern Europe in 1945, and the Hungarian Communist Party received 17% of the vote. In spite of their defeat, they started to gain control of law enforcement and established the political police, the AVH (later known as the AVO), and exercised increased pressure on the leading party. Industries were subsequently nationalized and religious organizations were banned. In 1947, the leaders in power were arrested and charged with "conspiracy against the Republic."

At the next parliamentary election in 1947, the Communists committed widespread election fraud but even so, they only managed to increase their share to 24% in the Parliament. Faced with their second failure at the polls, they changed tactics and—under new orders from Moscow—decided to eschew democratic facades and speed up the Communist takeover. In 1948, a new Communist party was created under the name of the Hungarian Working People's Party. Opposition parties were simply declared illegal, and additional leaders were arrested or forced into exile.

In 1949, the Parliament passed a new Constitution which was modeled after the Soviet Union's. The name of the country was changed to the People's Republic of Hungary, "the country of the workers and peasants" where "every authority is held by the working people." Socialism was declared to be the main goal of the nation. A new coat-of-arms was adopted with the Communist symbols of the red star and the hammer and sickle, and the oppressive Stalinist era began.

This was the beginning of an age when people regularly disappeared or were taken away indefinitely – all of which created a horribly fearful atmosphere. Taking advantage of the suppressed nation, the Communists started to confiscate private property throughout the entire country. When Ferenc understood what was happening to other people's farms nationwide, he dismantled most of their buildings on the ranch as well as part of their main house leaving the family with only one room and a kitchen. He sold all the used materials, such as the wood and tiles, and pocketed the money before the Communists could get their hands on it. When most of their land was confiscated by the beginning of the 1950s, the Gals had nothing left but two acres from what was precious and dear to them. The only additional thing they were allowed to keep was the remains of their home. The confiscated land went to the Communist collective, in Hungarian commonly referred to as the TSZ, and to its managers who, to add insult to injury, openly invaded the family's privacy by entering their tiny home without the Gals' invitation. Seeing strangers living on their previously owned land broke their hearts.

The Communists also confiscated the family's two remaining horses. At the time, the animals were valuable for two reasons: they provided mobility and were used for agricultural labor. Since the rest of the property wasn't theirs anymore, at the end of the year the family no longer had abundance of agricultural products, and their monetary compensation was not reflective of their hard labor done for the collective. Even though they still owned a reduced-size land, after the Communist takeover, there were times when the Gals had to go hungry. A new quota was established by the regime and there was a limit to how many animals they were allowed. The limits were based on the size of the family and it was far from generous. They were also not allowed to keep eggs, sugar, flour, or any excess food at home; it was now considered a crime. If they did find themselves having any extra, by law, they immediately had to offer and submit it to the nearest TSZ.

First the family had no choice but to accept the new status quo. However, Ida's father could not, in good conscious, watch his young children and wife starve so he did what needed to be done whether it was against the law or not. It was a risky idea given how small and visible their farm was but it sure didn't lack creativity! In their garden, there were many sizable haystacks from years back which shrank with time. He piled multiple heaps on top of each other to make them as high as possible. Then he cut an ample size circle in the middle leaving a thick enough wall all around that the center would be invisible and relatively soundproof. He then embarked on raising pigs, chickens, and turkeys in his one of a kind "courtyard" so he could feed his kids. By manipulating the system Ferenc risked being caught and imprisoned daily but the brave family man attempted to defy the odds.

FULFILLING MY AMERCIAN DREAM!

To keep his family away from the Communists who were in close proximity, he decided to move his clan from their ranch to their two-story city dwelling. Originally, the lower level was divided into a hog pen and a stable, and the upper level was the living quarters. Disregarding the layout, the Communists ordered Ida's family to hand over their second floor to a family they didn't even know, and from then on the Gals had to live downstairs. Ferenc did his best to convert the lower level and make it as inhabitable as humanly possible. The family of seven was now living in a bachelor space that consisted of one room and a kitchen; the toilet was outside. Eventually, Ida's father was able to save enough cash to pay off the people upstairs to move out and let the Gals re-inhabit their own property.

Ida—who was exceptionally sensitive to injustice—deep down was extremely disturbed by the events. The Communist takeover fueled Ida's anger and desperate desire to leave behind the regime to which she was unable to assimilate. Her compulsion to succeed elsewhere—especially after she witnessed what happened to her idolized role model, Lidia—was becoming ineradicable.

Since Communism was supposed to be a classless society, owning anything that was more upscale or expensive than your fellow man's possessions, was considered immoral and against the political climate. When Lidia's finer belongings—she earned with years of hard manual labor across the ocean—were confiscated by the police in front of her niece, they both felt crushed. Lidia now deeply regretted moving back to Hungary; her unrest grew exponentially, and she became determined to escape and return to America. Suspecting what Lidia was up to, Ida's thirst for America intensified.

Communism, as an atheist philosophy, denied the individual's liberty to practice religion. After the change, places of worship were closed, along with the schools that were on their property. Ida had started her elementary education at a Protestant institution that was next to the church where the Gals attended service. She continued to go to the same place until the new government put its hands on it. While this particular educational facility remained a school, the curriculum was redesigned and aligned with the administration's philosophy.

Life under oppression is extremely hard on any being. One way or another, everybody was monitored via a thorough spy system. It was not uncommon for individuals to be blackmailed into spying on their own relatives and children were often bribed to tell on their parents. Accordingly, one always had to watch what one said. Even jokes could be, and many times were, punished by imprisonment. The population now lived in constant fear and freedom of expression was completely diminished.

The habit of self-monitoring became many people's survival technique to avoid being beaten, interrogated, imprisoned, or hanged. It manifested in censoring not only what one did, said, but also with what one thought! The horrors of this era stayed with most people who had to live through it, including Ida. The fear got so ingrained in her, that it took years of conscious effort to stop her habit of watching oneself and only decades afterward did her nightmares go completely away.

One of the reasons one could be severely beaten was for one's heritage, namely, not being blue collar enough. If the AVO couldn't find a reason to hurt you, they just made one up. There was one horrific incident in the neighborhood after one of the men was declared to be a so-called kulak. The word originates from Russia; the kulaks were basically affluent peasants who were wealthy enough to own a farm and hire labor. Being a kulak was fundamentally treated as a sin against a Communist society and consequently many of them were arrested, exiled, or killed for the sheer reason that they owned more than most. Once the Gals' neighbor was declared to be one, the local authorities were looking for a reason to pick a fight with him so that they could finish him off. The police paid him a visit and noticed that the water dish of his sweet puppy happened to be empty. The Communists had already confiscated everything he owned, so there was nothing else to take, but there was one thing left to do: beat him to death. They bashed him brutally to the point that he passed out and then left him on the frozen ground in the middle of winter. Miraculously he did survive but he was never the same person again…

The Gals were kulaks themselves, so they had plenty to be worried about. They carefully had to navigate the political changes economically and emotionally. Nevertheless, Ida's parents were committed to not joining the Communist party. They tried to stay away from both, the ideology as well as the organization, as much as they could. However, Vilma's youngest sister was the village's post master and if she wanted to keep her job, she had to join the local chapter. Even though the Gals were tight-knit, not accepting what they considered selling her soul, they all distanced themselves from her. Matter of fact, the family went even a step further and disowned her. While Ida's mother did talk to her briefly, once in a while, the sister was no longer a welcomed member of their circle.

FULFILLING MY AMERCIAN DREAM!

Meanwhile, in the midst of increasingly limited personal freedom and entrepreneurship, Ida, as a young teenager, started working as a water waitress at the collective. She carried refreshments to the dozens of laborers who were working on the fields in exchange for some pocket money which she happily spent on her wardrobe. Not even the debilitating impact of the dictatorship was able to kill this opportunity-seeking, budding business woman's spirit.

Ida's education was atypical compared to most pupils. After she finished elementary school, she went to a trade school focusing on various administrative skills such as typing. However, her economically challenged parents could not afford it, so she had to stop for more than a year. During her time off, her academic interests changed, and she decided to focus more on industrial subjects, so in the fall of 1956 she enrolled into another trade school where her interest in business was going to be nurtured. However, history interfered with her plans.

FULFILLING MY AMERCIAN DREAM!

The Street of Flirt

(Meeting Steve)

In the beginning of October 1956, Ida suffered a major loss. Her beloved aunt, Lidia, passed away. Perhaps she was the only one who truly understood Ida's thirst for America and freedom and Lidia left this Earth not knowing that she missed her window of opportunity to escape by only two weeks…

Around that time, Ida was out riding her bicycle in the fields and something very unusual happened: she looked up at the sky and a small airplane was dropping thousands of foreshadowing political flyers tied in bales and depicting a political caricature: the country's dictator, Matyas Rakosi, was running away from the infamous falling statue of Stalin that stood in Budapest. Under the picture it said in Hungarian: "You can try to run, you can try to escape, but you can't avoid your fate."

Ida was dying of curiosity and couldn't wait to examine the packages. She looked around carefully several times to make sure no one saw her picking one of the bundles up. She was old enough to know that what she was doing could have detrimental consequences: her parents would have been taken away if anyone noticed Ida was reading such anti-government material. The daring and radical drawing shocked her! She was fully aware that she could not share her feelings with Ferenc and Vilma. She suspected something serious was in the air and to protect them from what she witnessed she pedaled over to the neighbor's son. The brave 25-year old man already was a regular listener of Radio Free Europe—another forbidden outlet at the time. Ida knew he could confide in him, show him the flyers, and after conversing with him for a while, she also told him her deepest secrets of all: one day she wanted to go to America.

On October 23, 1956, when Ida was 17 years old, a revolution against the severe Soviet oppression erupted. The freedom fight was started by passionate and enthusiastic university students who protested the government and their street demonstration quickly

attracted thousands. The 82-foot-tall Stalin monument that Ida saw

on the flyers was demolished in the capital's city park, leaving

only his boots and the base. People cut out the imprinted insignia,

hammer and sickle, from the national flag leaving a hole in the

middle. The revolt swiftly spread not just nationwide but beyond

Hungary's borders, and became the first major threat to the USSR

since World War II. For a few days, Hungary, a tiny nation in

Europe, militarily defeated the enormous Soviet Union, and

Hungary's communist government collapsed.

By this time, the prisons were primarily packed with anti-

Communist political prisoners, not with real criminals. The

revolutionaries released them and suddenly there was a flood of

people who were rushing towards the Western border, in spite of it

being filled with mines. Those who stayed and tried to fight the

oppression did so with Molotov cocktails and rifles, eventually

realized they had no chance. The insurgents knew well that even

the slightest participation in the revolution would likely result in capital punishment, so many of them headed toward Austria. Those who simply had had enough and could no longer live in a dictatorship that violated any imaginable human right, also packed their bags. The mass exodus grew to a critical level.

Around that time, Ida happened to see her young neighbor again who told her what was going on outside of Gyoma. Having heard the news, her eyes opened wide because she immediately knew that this was the very moment she too could escape. Her moment of the life-time opportunity to leave the oppressive Communist regime behind had finally arrived!

She ran home to tell her sister she wanted go as soon as possible but first she had to figure out how. Up to that point she had never travelled! Not only had she never been abroad, she hardly ever went beyond her own town. To this farm girl the Austrian border seemed as far away as the end of the World.

FULFILLING MY
AMERCIAN DREAM!

As luck would have it—as Ida was trying to put together her master plan—she happened to see Steve on the street, a young man whom she knew vaguely but hadn't seen in a while. She remembered her classmate mentioning that he asked about her a while back, when he saw Ida riding her bicycle around town in her sporty, dark blue outfit with a baby blue scarf in her hair, and that Steve also mentioned that he was "keeping an eye" on Ida… While that sounded like he had a crush on her, she didn't give him her attention since previously she had also seen him taking a stroll with another young lady. Ida did know that Steve worked in Tokod, a miniscule town close to Budapest, and for the past two years he was fulfilling his duty for his mandatory, three-year military service in Western Hungary. She heard through the grapevine that he worked as a medical assistant in the ER and on oil-drilling projects in Lepseny, a village near the Austrian border. During his service, Steve got familiar with the area: he knew the larger towns, the smaller villages, some of the farms, and most importantly had an idea how to escape, although this was not something of which Ida was aware. He also knew how to bribe the border-guarding officers and of which individuals he had to be wary.

That morning, when Ida and Steve by chance walked towards each other on the street, he said hi to the fair-skinned, green-eyed, Nordic blonde beauty, but she didn't respond; she was lost in her thoughts. Only after a few steps did it registered that she forgot to reply to his hello. She suddenly turned around and with a delay greeted him. She did so because she was a polite young lady, but the truth was she was not interested in him—not only because she thought he was taken, but because he was too handsome and way too elegantly dressed. He was also too muscular due to his military training and regular swimming workouts in Lake Balaton. In addition, she heard that he had worked in the capital beforehand and that had its own stigma especially from a peasant girl's perspective. As far as Ida was concerned, he looked like a vain baron in his pricey outfit. Rumor had it that he spent all his money on his stylish clothes. Plus, he was five years older than she was and all the local girls were crazy about him. Ida had the impression that he was a womanizer and she most definitely didn't want to deal with that down the line!

At any rate, after Ida returned Steve's hello, he asked her whether she was interested in having coffee with him right then and there. Even though she had all those not so flattering ideas in her head about him, she, for no particular reason, ended up accepting his invite. After their morning rendezvous he walked her home and invited her to the local dance hall at the cultural center. However, no dancing was going taking place that night. Instead, the excited young men and women of the town were going collect donations and food for the freedom fighters. Ida was very interested regardless of the fact that there was another man, Sandor, with whom she had already been on three dates. They saw each other infrequently since he worked in the city and he only visited Gyoma once in a while. Their relationship was neither serious nor committed. As a matter of fact, at one point she had already turned him down. During their last date, he too told her that he wanted to leave the country even though he had no idea how to execute his idea. That day Sandor happened to be in town again and asked Ida out for the same evening; they were supposed to meet in front of the church. However, the young lady got far more interested in aiding the freedom fighters. She also felt he was invested in her enough so as she was rushing to the dance hall and saw Sandor waiting for her, instead of offending him again and turning him down one more time, she decided not to put him in an awkward position and instead went to meet up with Steve.

Wanting to contribute to the success of the uprising her own way, Ida arrived at the meeting with goodies that she secretly took from their pantry that her mother refilled just days before, so they wouldn't immediately notice. Once they gathered, the local youth talked about the country's struggle for freedom and need for independence, and then got a truck to transport the collected food supply to the revolutionaries. That was the night the topic of leaving the country first came up between Ida and Steve. He confessed that he wanted to escape from Hungary without his relatives knowing about it and he detailed his plan of getting to the

FULFILLING MY AMERCIAN DREAM!

West. At the time, admitting such to an acquaintance was risky and could have resulted in the death penalty. When the excited Ida asked Steve whether he was nervous, he said "Yes!" and his humility made him even more relatable. Without thinking much about it, right then and there, Ida chose the man with whom she trusted her milestone journey. He was smart, strong, and she instinctually knew that if it ever came to push comes to shove, he would not leave her out in the cold. "I want to go with you." she said; he smiled and then nodded. Ida was upfront with him and shared her concern that she didn't have any money. She didn't want to be a burden to him, but Steve didn't seem to be worried. He assured her not to worry about it—he had enough for them both. That sealed the deal between them, and their bond was formed.

Steve detailed that he not only wanted to leave the country, but if he wanted to stay alive, he *had* to leave the country. Steve felt that due to his patriotic activity during the revolution, he had no other choice but to go abroad. When the uprising broke out, he and his other buddies climbed into the lake villa of Matyas Rakosi and distributed all the edibles they found to the starving masses. The unusual thing about the vacation home was that the Communist dictator had a refrigerator in most of the rooms and all of them were stacked with a variety of alcohol and such rare food specialties that most people not only hadn't eaten but have never even heard of. The exotic found tropical fruits when passed out were not recognized by the locals as food. By offering the tyrant's supplies to the locals, Steve became both a hero of the revolution and the enemy of the state. Fully knowing that by the country's recent laws he committed a crime, Steve with two of his freedom fighter collaborators, forced their superior to release them from the military at gun point along with their army ID. It was crucial that they obtain their documentation so they could identify themselves to the authorities at anytime. Lack of ability to provide credentials would have resulted in being arrested on the spot.

After meeting Steve twice in one day, Ida reiterated to her sister, Irene, that she wanted to leave Hungary promptly. The next day,

FULFILLING MY AMERCIAN DREAM!

Ida suggested to Steve to come over to their house for dinner. An invitation from a young woman to one's home so rapidly was quite unusual and not exactly customary. As a matter of fact, it was quite a big deal, but Ida didn't have a minute to waste. Although Steve was caught off guard, he accepted.

Because the families knew each other, Ida's mother was not worried at a bit about having the young man over. As it turned out, Ida's mom happened to know Steve well since his belated mother, who passed away when he was just a six-year old boy, were on good terms. In addition, Vilma and Steve's stepmother were cousins and that is why Steve trusted Ida from the get-go. In a small village such relations were important; it put people on their best behavior and that generated a sense of safety for everyone.

According to regional winter customs, just days before the Gals had held a Hungarian style pig luau as they had a fair amount of blood sausages, rich bacon, smoked ham, peasant style black pudding, and fresh cabbage to share. While today these foods may seem like protein galore, at the time, especially for those who did agricultural and physical labor outside all day, these were greatly appreciated and popular dishes.

Ida's sister, Irene, and her fiancé, John became anxious about leaving. The four of them got together and started to carefully plan their escape. After the dinner with their parents, Ida, Irene, Steve, and John, moved into the living room, closed all the doors to ensure Ferenc and Vilma wouldn't have a chance to hear their important conversation. None of them had any idea how to go about the escape except Steve who sounded, composed, perceptive, and confident. By the end of the evening they had a plan! Irene put her clothes in their parents' suitcase, Ida too threw in a few pieces, and then they gave it to Steve. The reason Ida hardly packed anything was because she only had a few worthless items. On the other hand, Irene had a collection of Western garments that was too gorgeous to leave behind in Gyoma. They told Vilma that he needed to borrow their empty luggage because he was going to take food to his aunt in the capital. Unlike today when everyone travels and has bags at home, that was not the case during the Communist era. People were forbidden to travel not only internationally but many times locally. The excuse made sense to Ida's mother and Steve went off with the portmanteau hiding the girls' belongings.

Once both men hit the road, the sisters wrote a letter to their parents detailing why they were leaving and gave the note to their cousin to hand it to Vilma several hours after they took off. They wanted to make sure that by that time their parents got the envelope, they were already far enough away. They also made their kin swear that she would not tell anyone that they left for at least two weeks. In their farewell summary, they specifically asked their parents not to look for them and gave their word that they would send a sign of life as soon as they crossed over to Austria. Ida and Irene also made their kin swear that she would not tell anyone for at least two weeks later that they had left for the West. Before her trip, Ida took the time to pay a visit to all of her family members and friends; in her heart she wanted to say good bye to

them all.

FULFILLING MY AMERCIAN DREAM!

The Divine Journey of Paprika Spiked Brown

(The Escape)

Once the big day arrived, they started to get ready. The trade school Ida attended was in a neighboring city and every morning she had to take the train quite early. The school was on hiatus due to the upheaval, but she didn't tell Vilma that, so Ida left for the railway station as she would every day. Irene was working as a secretary in the neighboring town and she too commuted by train daily. So, the sisters left together, and their mother didn't question it since everything seemed as usual. If Vilma even had the tiniest hunch, she would never have allowed them to defect.

Irene's fiancé lived in a nearby village, called Korosladany. The grand plan was that John would arrive to Gyoma's railway station at 7 AM by train, the four of them would meet up, and then then they would take off for Budapest. From there the quartet would continue traveling to the Austrian border and, with Steve's guidance, they would cross to the west.

FULFILLING MY AMERCIAN DREAM!

When Ida, Irene, and Steve got the terminal, it was announced that due to additional strikes no trains were running in the area that day. Therefore, Irene's fiancé, John, was stuck at home, could not adhere to their arrangement, and wouldn't be able to meet them. Ida definitely did not want to go back home since she had already bid her farewell to everyone and she was not going to miss the opportunity to join a person who knew exactly how to escape. Neither did Steve, since he needed to hurry if he didn't want to be caught by the military forces. On the other hand, Irene said that she would not leave without John, so she decided to stay behind.

Steve gave Irene his aunt's address in Budapest and told her that they would wait for Irene and John for 3 days there. If they hadn't arrived by that time, Ida and Steve would leave for Austria. Budapest was full of Soviet soldiers again just like during World War II and that was the maximum amount of time they could wait. So, on that cold December morning, Ida and Steve started to walk along the railroads to the next town, Mezotur, which was about 14 miles away.

At first, Irene didn't go back to see her folks. Instead she started to march in the direction where her fiancé lived. Irene walked for a long time but Korosladany was just too far. Fortunately, an old man with a tractor offered to take her to where she was going and finally, she arrived at John's place safely. By this time, Ida's cousin had already given the letter to their mother and she was beside herself thinking that both of her daughters were gone.

In the meantime, Ida and Steve reached Mezotur by early afternoon—a long day without stopping to eat or drink anything. There wasn't a soul at the railway station. However, the building was open, so they went in hoping that possibly a train would come and take them to Budapest. They sat down and ate some of the sausages that Steve had brought with him in his briefcase that was filled with nothing but tasty country wurst and they were able to get some tap water from the fountain.

FULFILLING MY
AMERCIAN DREAM!

While they were sitting there, unexpectedly a train arrived from the opposite direction and a familiar person got off. He entered the hall where they were having their humble lunch—it turned out to be Ida's neighbor's husband, a high-ranking Communist officer...

They both got anxious especially when he approached them and bombarded them with several questions. They were both afraid that perhaps he suspected their plans. They also wondered why he himself was there. It seemed odd that he was heading home, given that he was stationed somewhere else and there also was a revolution everywhere. Ida and Steve shared with him that they were going to Budapest to help out his famished relatives because during the fights it was hard to obtain food in the big city. Thankfully, he seemed to believe them, perhaps because in the countryside and small communities straight and honest talk was the custom. Not only did he seem to believe them, he was even helpful: he told them that there was a train coming soon and was headed in the direction of the capital.

After a few minutes later, Ida and Steve were elated to hear the loud speaker broadcasting the train's arrival. The announcer warned the travelers that it would only be there for a few minutes, so Steve ran to buy tickets for both of them. He then gave Ida hers so that they could travel apart in case he got caught by the authorities. Not to worry though, he'd always be close and would find her when it was time.

The rail took them to Szolnok, a county seat of the region—now they were definitely on their way to Budapest! There they had to wait for another connection. Since Ida was travelling penniless, Steve again bought their passage. He had more money with him than usual because he had just inherited some cash from his grandfather who had recently passed away in a nearby town, Gyula, and he picked up his inheritance before they had left. They continued to travel separately; he seemed concerned for her safety and never wanted to put her in danger. This was especially important now because the upheaval in the country left most of the trains empty and it wasn't easy to blend in. People were too timid to leave their residence unless they were heading toward Austria. Steve wanted to make sure that no one put two and two together.

He also knew that if he got caught, he would be sentenced to death.

He was worried that the military police had already been after him,

but he didn't know for sure. Given all of the chaos in the country,

he was hoping that they were not yet actively searching for him. At

the time, without much technology, locating an individual was a

far slower process than it is these days. It took three to four months

for officials to realize who was where and who was missing.

It was nearly 5 AM the next day when they arrived at the capital.

Due to the curfew they couldn't leave the railway station until 8

AM. Having nothing else to do, they finished the sausages. In Pest,

they tried to find their way to the Eighth District where Steve's

aunt lived. As a result of the fighting, the city was full of corpses

covered with newspapers and those who were desperately looking

for their loves ones, had to lift the paper sheets off the dead bodies

to identify them. If Ida and Steve wanted to reach their destination,

they had to carefully step over the disintegrating human

skeletons—a highly disturbing maneuver Ida still remembers.

FULFILLING MY AMERCIAN DREAM!

Steve's aunt, Gitta, and his uncle, Laszlo, were both extremely welcoming. They didn't have any children of their own and so they felt quite enchanted by Ida—so much so, that they sort of fell in love with her. Being sweet individuals, they wanted Ida to stay with them in Budapest and not leave with Steve. They told Ida that once Steve made a lot of money in the West, he could send for her, but Ida declined. Then the deeply religious aunt Gitta hung a pendant, depicting the Virgin Mary, on a thin thread, instead of a metal chain, and placed it around Ida's neck. Gitta strongly believed that the medal would guard Ida on her journey and from that moment on, she was convinced of its protective power herself, even though, at the time, she was not religious at all. The medallion was not valuable since it was made of aluminum, nevertheless it erased all Ida's fears.

She knew the trip ahead would be dangerous and many people had already been shot or blown up. However, she really took to heart the message the aunt had conveyed and anchored herself in the feeling that nothing bad was going to happen them.

Ida told Gitta that when she arrived in America and would have enough money, she'd buy the same medal made of gold and wear it for the rest of her life. While she kept the original one, she did eventually buy an identical pendant made of precious metal and has had it around her neck ever since. It has given Ida strength throughout the years and even today the pendant means the world to her. Generous Aunt Gitta, also gave Ida a large, valuable tablecloth to take with her to America without which Ida may not have made it to the Austrian border…

Ida and Steve waited 72 hours, but Irene and John never arrived. Not being able to communicate with them in any way, on the fourth day, when it was still dark, they left. Budapest originally consisted of two cities: Buda on the west side of the Danube and Pest, where Aunt Gitta lived, on the east side. They had to cross over to the other side of the wide river so that they could start moving in the right direction.

FULFILLING MY AMERCIAN DREAM!

First, they took a train to Vasvar, a town in Western Hungary, about nine miles from the border. The ride seemed to take forever even though in actuality it only lasted a few hours. The rails were completely full; there was no room to sit down or to move much at all. Close to half of the passengers intended to leave the country and everybody looked incredibly nervous. People were extraordinarily careful about how they communicated, they spoke cryptically, and were trying to be as diplomatic as possible. No one dared to ask another traveler whether they too were trying to escape.

Based on Ida's observation, the AVO was not yet looking for Steve. Nevertheless, he was remarkably concerned, so he maintained his physical distance from Ida. He encountered two anti-Communist brothers who—as political prisoners—just got out of jail. Steve suspected they were trying to leave just like most of them, so he inquired whether they were "visiting the area" but Steve's ironed, CIA agent-like clothes was confusing to the men and suddenly they acted jumpy. They feared that officials were already tracking them, and their suspicion grew. In order to derail the dialogue, they attempted to find out where he was heading, and whether he was travelling alone. He said he was "doing what they were doing" and no, he was not traveling alone but with his comely fiancé. In actuality, Ida was not even his girlfriend and there was no romantic relationship between them. However, Steve was falling for her, so the thought of Ida being with him came easily. The brothers still didn't believe Steve, so they insisted on him introducing Ida to them. Due to the brothers' request Steve took them to the front of the train and introduced them. Once the former prisoners chatted with innocent Ida, they calmed down, and no longer hesitated to open up to Steve.

They revealed that they obtained all kinds of weapons to protect themselves and headed for the West as hastily as they could. They each had four grenades on both sides of the inside of their coats, as well as ammunition and pistols. These two were certainly not to be provoked.

FULFILLING MY AMERCIAN DREAM!

Shortly before approaching the final destination, the porter whispered to the crowd: "If you want to go any further than Vasvar, you'll have the opportunity to hop off the moving train when it slows down which will still be far away from the station…" He obviously knew what was going on and where people were heading but he too had to be careful about how to phrase things. Most Hungarians who stayed behind were more than sympathetic towards those who decided to escape. Many of them encouraged the refugees and some went out of their way to help them.

Getting off the train before it got to its final destination was crucial because Vasvar was overrun with authorities, police, and secret police—people escapees didn't want to encounter. Border reinforcement was strong and Soviet check points more frequent than usual, especially along the Austrian border.

The conditions were snowy and slushy when the train slowed down. Ida jumped out from the front of the train and Steve from the back into a frozen canal. There were many others who got off early including the brothers who invited the young couple to spend the night at their friend's house. They had a plan already in place not only for that night but for the entire escape. They knew exactly how they would get over to the other side, and they also had plenty of money which always could come in handy. Steve told Ida that they were going to stick with the well-supplied men all the way to Austria.

The four of them walked to a small town where they met up with some allies who took the small group in where they could spend the next day. Just like Ida's father did when he was escaping from the Soviets, they had to wait for nighttime so that no one would notice them while moving towards their target. Once dawn was approaching, they stopped at another ranch, rested, and then waited for nightfall before getting on the road again.

During their trip they didn't have the opportunity to shower or change. For a winter voyage that took them through forests, farms, and rough areas, Ida wasn't particularly well equipped. Since she had to leave home in an outfit that would have been appropriate for school, Ida couldn't bring thick and layered winter wear. Instead she was wearing only a light jacket and thin-soled shoes. In addition to her school bag, the only thing she could sneak out with her was her simple brown purse. Luckily, Steve had thought about their journey carefully, wore sturdy army boots, and brought an extra pair that he could give Ida to wear.

All the farmers in the area were aware that all these people were trying to leave the country, as did the authorities and the occupying forces, and there were many police raids both day and night. Nevertheless, most farmers courageously hid them in their barns among the livestock where no one would search for them. Each night when they walked for miles in the cold, they were risking their lives. No one was safe but that's exactly how revolutions and escapes usually take place. Their group stayed out of the cities and high traffic areas and was always hyper aware of their surroundings . The second place they arrived at was already full of others from all over the country. These farms became growing hubs for the refugees where everyone was suspicious of everyone else; they obsessively sized each other up.

Ida and Steve had slept at three different meeting points by the time they reached their destination. At their last stop, there were already 27 men, women, and children waiting to cross over. The guides waited for enough people to gather before leading them forward. Instead of taking two to three people, they required a group of 20 people at least to make it financially worthwhile for them take such a substantial risk.

Ida's and Steve's guide, who lived on the property of their third stop, knew the area well and had already assisted other groups to escape Hungary before them. He asked everyone to put all their jewelry, money, valuables, and everything that was worth anything on the large dinner table covered with a big top sheet. He was not afraid to take everything from everybody as a payment for him to help them defect. Since Ida didn't have anything valuable on her except Gitta's flawless, champagne, damask tablecloth, she put

that on the pile.

After everyone had handed over all of their possessions something

unexpected happened. A jealous neighbor—knowing that the guide

was making a lot of money—came over and grabbed off of the

table everything he could and said: "I am the one who will take all

what's here. Otherwise I'll report you all to the AVO!" People got

outraged and unnerved that he was indeed going to turn them in.

Ida's and Steve's new buddies calmly said to the neighbor: "Look,

can you be fair about this and discuss it?" Then one of the brothers

put his arm around him and they shepherded him outside and shot

him! When the men came back in, one of the brothers said to the

group: "OK, everyone! Everything is taken care of and we should

be able to leave now."

Before they left, one of the brothers opened his coat and showed

everyone his grenades, pistols, and weapons he was carrying, and

then announced: "I want you all to know that I paid the most amount of money to the guide, so I'm the boss. If you want to join me, you can but if anyone comes close to me or does anything tricky, I'll shoot you. Are we all clear?" Everybody was and off they went to pursue the border bridge to freedom. Before they proceeded, Ida broke off a last piece of Hungarian pine branch hoping to celebrate Christmas with it in Austria.

Their journey was not easy. There were refugees who could handle the systematic march better than others, but they all tried to support each another. There was a family of six with two old people who were too exhausted and could not keep up, so Ida and Steve volunteered to carry the kids around their necks so the parents could attend to the grandparents. If they didn't want to leave them behind, the only option was to take on their load.

Ida knew that the forest close to the border was full of landmines. Maybe for that reason, she was on autopilot, emotionless, and incredibly focused. She was keeping her eyes on the prize and nothing was going to faze her. She was extraordinarily determined and had a feeling that she was soon going to be free.

Eventually, they got to a small but speedy river with a bridge above it guarded by a Hungarian and Soviet solider. This was going to be it… But first, they had to find a way to convince the latter to let them escape on the bridge or if they didn't get shot by the men, they would have had to swim across in the rushing icy water.

Ida's and Steve's smuggler told the group to stay quietly behind in the woods and to not move until he returned. Then pretending to be drunk, he went up to the men and whispered to the Hungarian one to let his people cross. After he learned how many of them there were, he told he guard to wait while he took his partner for a 20 minute walk… 15 minutes later he returned without the Russian and the group was told to rush over to Austria. From her Bible studies, Ida remembered the story of the parting of the Red Sea. She felt, instead of a large body of water, God opened a special path for her, and she was able to walk across the bridge without any harm.

After several days of travel, on December 11, in the midst of cheering Western border guards, Ida and Steve finally arrived at their next destination: Austria.

FULFILLING MY AMERCIAN DREAM!

CHAPTER THREE

The Camp of Blush Nude

(Austria: December, 1956 – February, 1957)

3. Austria: December, 1956 – February, 1957

Once Ida got to the other side, her tears started to fall. She felt so much joy that she wanted to shout from the bottom of her lungs, but the moment was just too overwhelming.

Having left oppression behind, Ida immediately felt safe being on Austrian soil. The Western welcome was warm and accommodating; big trucks were waiting to take them to shelter.

Ida and Steve climbed up into the vehicle and were taken to the next village where a school building was set up for them. The locals immediately brought them food and they were able to freshen up and shower. The Salvation Army and the Red Cross brought them warm clothes into which they changed. The humanitarian organizations made sure they were appropriately supplied with medication and food. In addition, they got a first aid kit, chocolate, a small amount of pocket money, and—as gracious hosts of the era—they even made sure those who smoked had plenty of cigarettes on hand.

The Jewish Hungarian family, whose children Steve and Ida carried for miles in the woods, was finally safe as well. Luckily, the Israeli league too was organized, and upon their arrival, they received many forms of generous assistance. At last they were able to put the horrors of the last decade and a half behind.

After taking care of the refugees' immediate needs, the officials designated a specific refugee camp, "lager" as they said in German, to each individual. When Ida and Steve arrived to theirs, they received the Hungarian welcome: raw moonshine! Already in the lager, the inhabitants who were waiting for their transit to the next country, shared their own bottle freely and joyously as they celebrated with the newcomers. For their toast, Ida and Steve only had a couple of sips of fruit brandy but that night they got drunk on life and freedom!

The town, Feffernitz, was in the Southern part of Austria, close to the Slovenian and Italian border, and had picturesque mountains as a backdrop. The small city was the site of a post World War II British sector displaced persons camp that was turned into a 1956 refugee camp that housed them. The rooms in the barracks were suitable for two to four people. The interior was simple and poorly furnished but civilized, nonetheless. There was a bed, a wood stove, a table, and a couple of chairs, but no curtains on the windows. The toilets were outside the buildings, and there were water wells just like back in the farm in Gyoma.

Every winter morning approximately 500 escapees stood in line outside to pick up their meal which consisted of the same thing: coffee, two slices of bread, and a piece of cheese. It was Ida who always picked up the couple's breakfast and brought it back to their place so they could eat together. During these outings, Ida noticed that people were getting irritated with the unfamiliar taste and were bored of the same exact menu day after day. Many started to throw their yellow pieces of cheese away the moment they got them. Being the budding entrepreneur Ida already was, she immediately got an idea! When someone was about to throw their share away, she asked whether she could have it. She ended up collecting a large amount of dairy which she then took to the nearby village and asked whether they would be willing to exchange it for eggs, bacon, and other delicacies. Once she started to accumulate an excess of those delicacies, taking resourcefulness to a new level, Ida then sold the surplus to the refugees in the lager or exchanged them for household items that she and Steve needed.

Not long after Ida left Gyoma, there was real chaos in the Gal household. Vilma worried herself not knowing her daughters' whereabouts and had a nervous breakdown. However, when Irene reappeared their mother was ecstatic that at least one of her children hadn't left after all. On the other hand, Vilma was distressed because Ida departed with a man to whom she was not married. During the 1950's that was not only looked down upon, but it was downright shameful and scandalous for a decent and young woman who was raised to follow strict religious customs.

Irene, now under her parents' supervision, had her own worries as well. She was genuinely afraid to initiate her escape and leave her mother behind in such a condition. Gathering all her courage, she invited her fiancé over to their house but that didn't go particularly well… Vilma lost control, physically attacked John, spat on him, and blamed him for his failed "bride kidnapping." She couldn't stand the idea of losing not one but two daughters about the same time and possibly never seeing them again. Given the Communist travel ban at the time, this was a real possibility and hard for a mother to handle. It took a while for Vilma to calm down and reevaluate.

Meanwhile, as promised in her letter, Ida was trying to find a way to inform her family that she was well and alive. At the time, the method people utilized to notify each other was via Radio Free Europe. They used code names so the Hungarian authorities could not track down neither the sender nor the recipient. Ida's cryptogram was "Lily of the Valley," a fragrant and delicate white flower she loved. While her relatives missed the broadcast, their radio-listening neighbor didn't, and—bless his heart—he passed on the message in the midst of Vilma's desperation.

After some time, their mother agreed to Irene's departure if Irene and John got married beforehand at the city hall. She wanted them to leave as husband and wife via Yugoslavia, which was, at that point, the only way to escape the country. The Austrian border was rumored to be no longer a viable option of escape because the political situation was escalating in Hungary and the control of the area kept increasing. They heard that the government was forcefully stopping the mass exodus via Austria; Irene and John needed to find another viable option. As soon as Irene and John became husband and wife during a speedy ceremony, they left their town behind.

FULFILLING MY AMERCIAN DREAM!

Vilma was losing sleep over Irene's flight, and rightfully so. While Ida's escape was relatively smooth a month before, Irene's was far more treacherous. As she was fleeing to Yugoslavia in January, while crossing the border, a woman was shot right next to her and she died on the spot. Witnessing a woman close to her age being murdered that close traumatized Irene. It took her a long time to overcome the nightmares that followed the manslaughter. Thank God, Irene was not hurt and with John made it safely to Yugoslavia.

Having heard the fantastic news, Ida decided to send the suitcase with Irene's clothes to the camp where she was staying along with some chic designer pieces Ida came across in the donation pile specifically dedicated to the refugees. Thanks to the Red Cross that acted as the era's reliable shipping agency, the sisters were able to communicate directly, exchange letters, and Ida was able to get Irene's wardrobe to her intact and on time.

FULFILLING MY AMERCIAN DREAM!

In the meantime, in Feffernitz, Ida and Steve were getting closer to each other and their romance gradually started to blossom. Steve's personality was not what Ida originally expected it to be. Instead, he was a good and funny man, a true comedian, and a real people person at heart. He loved everybody, enjoyed going to parties, and being social. He was also organized and orderly—not just with his clothing and immediate environment but he kept their living quarter that way too.

Unlike storybook romances, their relationship was not based on mad attraction and unstoppable thirst for each other but rather on a deep friendship and partnership. Out of the two, the extraverted Steve was much more romantic than the introverted Ida. One way he showed his feelings for her was by always taking care of her in every way he could. Ida noticed his never-ending and thoughtful care during their journey and their relationship began to evolve. First, they held hands, then their first kiss happened, and then he got the courage to tell her that he "liked" her. And, she said she "liked him" too! In these rather unusual circumstances, there was also another significant element to their growing closeness: they both felt that they honestly needed each other. Staying together was as much of an emotional decision as it was a practical necessity. Ida has always been rather logical and pragmatic in her thinking and it was an easy decision to stay with a man who was strong and brave, shared her cultural and regional heritage, and who was willing to go through thick and thin with her.

While waiting for their official documentation, the young couple got worrisome news. Steve was told that political police were looking for him in Hungary… Everybody knew they were not be trifled with and if they could not get to you directly, they would not hesitate to go after your family with full force. That was not the message Steve wanted to hear. The AVO—well known for its merciless torture techniques—pressured Steve's father to tell his son to come back. While they promised that nothing would happen to Steve, he knew better. So, it didn't even cross his mind, nevertheless, it was heartbreaking to hear that his relatives were interrogated for months. The AVO went as far as demanding that he not only trick Steve, but Ida as well, and lure them both into returning. While Ida never doubted her decision to leave nor entertained the idea to change her mind, she missed her family a lot, even though she was not homesick. Knowing how much Steve's relatives were made to suffer, her determination was reinforced a thousand times.

While Ida and Steve refused go back, there were others who gave in to the pressure. There was another young couple in the same barrack who eloped, but eventually ended up feeling so much remorse, they returned to where they came from.

On the other hand, our forward-looking pair had more ambitious plans. In the lager, there were some tremendously helpful elderly people who had have lived there since World War II. After escaping Hungary, they decided never to move on and that was fine with the authorities. They made Austria their new home so much so that they even forgot their mother tongue. However, their hearts remained open especially when they met a fellow country(wo)man. Among other things, they donated food to the couple regularly and one day Ida got something particularly useful: A Singer sewing machine! While the latter item was only a temporary loan, Ida saw infinite business possibilities in it that down the line she also could involve Steve. On the spot she decided to learn how to sew and utilized the opportunity within days.

Having access to the Red Cross' donation of clothes, she picked out big, colorful dresses, and made curtains for her own windows—cleverly—as a form of advertisement. It didn't even take hours before people noticed the lager's new vogue. They flooded Ida with questions such as: where she got the cheerful pieces from, how did she obtain the fabric, and so on. Of course, she was not foolish to tell them all the details only that she had made the curtains herself. Her first orders came in instantly— because even refugees needed some privacy that the barracks' panes didn't allow. Her job was made easier by the fact that all the windows in the lager were the same size, so she didn't have to tailor each drapery but instead, "industrialize" the manufacturing process. Interestingly enough, the more outrageous the prints and the textile pieces were, the more in demand they became! Within weeks after springing into action and opening her first small business, Ida had more Austrian Schillings in her pocket than one would expect from a 17-year old refugee who had arrived without a penny.

Ida's creative thinking didn't stop there. Every barrack had a stove though not an electric one. It needed to be stoked manually so that it would heat up the place; however, the refugees were not getting enough wood and coal from the management to keep them warm. Finding dried wood in the middle of the winter was not an easy task and collecting smaller pieces around the lager on a daily basis was a bit too tedious for Ida who was becoming known for her efficiency and ambitious ideas.

Then Ida heard that in the nearby mountains, authorities were cutting down sky-high evergreen trees and chopping them into two or three logs. So, she came up with the solution to their heating problem! Ida suggested to Steve that they hike up all the way to the top and attempt to locate the cleared areas and then drag some of the pieces back with them to the lager. But the question remained: how? These were not easily movable but rather gigantic chunks. So, every morning, Steve and Ida would head up to the tall peaks and hike all day to find adequately dried wood that would burn well. Simultaneously, Ida convinced a neighbor to loan her a sleigh that in her mind would function as a simplified transportation vehicle. Once they found a right piece, they loaded it on the sled and did their best to force it to slide.

One day Ida found a massive cut that was the biggest she had yet seen. It was too large to place it on the sleigh, so she insisted that Steve sit on the oversized log and "drive" it down the hill while she balanced the sled packed with firewood. Due to its size, he tried to talk her out of it, but she would not let go. All she could think about was how warm it would keep them for weeks, so she wanted to get that log to the lager no matter what it took! Steve told her she was crazy, as its measures prevented them to have any control over its movement, but she said if he was not willing to do it, she would! And she did! They agreed that Steve would "operate" the sledge ahead of Ida and she would steer the timber. As they were approaching the village and the mountain was getting steeper, Ida literally started to fly just a bit too fast…. She was unable to "break" or slow down the airborne and speeding chunk so it read-ended Steve with such force he slid through the entire lager like a rocket. Thank heaven neither Steve nor anyone else got hurt, and Ida's laugh echoed in the valley for miles.

After the funny incident, Ida located two strong men with whom she made a deal: if they chopped up the gigantic blocks, half of it would be theirs and the other half would be Ida's and Steve's. A borrowed saw was put to use and soon they had more than an adequate amount of firewood. Life was suddenly cozy and warm, and instead of having to be out in the cold daily, they could now spend some of their mornings lounging around.

That, of course, didn't mean that they would not go on hikes for fun. Given that the majority of refugees were primarily young and full of vitality, they often explored the Alps and enjoyed the outdoors together.

One day a group decided to play tag out in the forest and in the midst of it all, Ida suddenly noticed that not one, but three guys were chasing her. So, she kept running even faster, as a matter of fact she sped up not realizing this was now no longer part of the game. She only got suspicious when they started to shout "Stop!" and their yelling turned into screaming. Fear hit her, and she grabbed onto a small tree as she was running too fast to come to a halt on her own. As her body jerked from the instant stop, it circled around the tree. She looked down and there was a vast vertical cliff under her feet, and the tree she was holding onto was the last scrub. Unbeknownst to her, the area was part of a mine and she almost dropped into it. If she took one more step, she would have probably fallen deep enough to break her spine.

FULFILLING MY AMERCIAN DREAM!

This was not the only occasion that Ida had a close call while there. Sometimes, just two of them would wonder off to the snowy woods and enjoy nature. One day on their way home, Ida was energetically jumping from one tree to another to decrease her downhill speed. Steve was just a bit further down standing at the bottom of the trail as he witnessed Ida grab onto a tree that was completely dry, and it broke in half. She lost her balance and tumbled twice in the air, just like a real acrobat, miraculously landing on her feet exactly in front of her boyfriend. Steve shocked and frozen by what he had just seen and was relieved when a second later the vivacious young gal burst into a reverberating laughter.

They weren't the only couple taking advantage of the beautiful environment the lager provided, though some tried to enjoy beauty in a different way. Theft and safety weren't concerning issues, however, there were a lot of single women around, so the Hungarians decided to unite their forces to ensure decent behavior and appointed an older man as a security guard. No one knew why

FULFILLING MY AMERCIAN DREAM!

his nickname was Uncle Speedy but eventually they all found out. He was particularly fast when it came to monitor and disrupting women of a certain kind… He did not hesitate to break up any l'amour that was temporary and paid. Ida later heard that he penned a memoir candidly exposing what he witnessed in the lager. He gave his book an amusing title: *Sweet Memories of Feffernitz - Uncle Speedy's Stories of Skirt Chasing.*

While there, all so called "1956ers" had to request a transfer to another country as Austria was beyond overwhelmed with close to 200,000 Hungarians seeking asylum. Ida chose and she signed up for the U.S.A. multiple times. She definitely didn't want to go anywhere else and she was very excited and hopeful about her destination. However, for the moment, they were directed to the Netherlands.

CHAPTER FOUR

The Country of Ladylike Pink

(Netherlands: March, 1957 – May, 1957)

4. <u>Netherlands: March, 1957 – May, 1957</u>

Upon arrival to the Netherlands, both Ida and Steve had to go through many of the same meticulous medical tests, including an x-ray, they already had in Austria. While waiting for their American entry visa Steve was told that he was diagnosed with tuberculosis, commonly known as TB, a bacterial infectious disease of the lungs. As a teenager who hadn't had enough biology studies yet, Ida first incorrectly suspected that he may have contracted the illness during a fire back in an Austrian restaurant where Steve, along with another Hungarian, bravely ran in to save the jukebox from the flames.

FULFILLING MY AMERCIAN DREAM!

Steve's sickness was especially scary since his mom as well as Ida's mother's sisters had had the same disease. During World War II, the two aunts were taken away to dig ditches for the Soviets. The forced labor took place outside during the freezing winter months and the cold most likely lowered their immune system. First, they contracted pneumonia and then TB. Eventually, all three women died so this was as daunting a news for them as it could get. Steve was immediately sent to a sanatorium, and the lovebirds got separated.

Ida was relocated to another refugee camp in a picturesque, small city called Zierikzee, 19 miles southwest of Rotterdam. The old, historic town received its city status in 1248 and was located on an island; it was a home to only a few thousand friendly inhabitants. Ida adored the place, but her heart was still set on the New World. She wasn't planning to stay in the Netherlands for more than a few months but first she had to wait for America's response to her immigration request.

FULFILLING MY AMERCIAN DREAM!

With the help of nurses provided by the ever-present Red Cross, Ida regularly visited Steve in the hospital. They would pick her up every weekend and take her to her boyfriend who was hours away. Then they would wait for her and once she finished spending time with Steve, they would give her a ride back to the camp. When the Red Cross realized that they were Hungarians—given the world's more than positive response to the courageous Hungarian Revolution of 1956—they would be even more helpful. They offered so much assistance to her that if she didn't experience all the benefits herself, she wouldn't have believed it. Given their ongoing and always generous aid, Ida swore that as soon as she was in a financial position, she would write a regular check to them. She later extended her commitment to the Salvation Army as well, since that was another organization that would be infinitely helpful throughout their years of hardship.

By the time Ida and Steve were in Holland, they were both able to write to their parents directly. Vilma was upset with Ida because she learned that she still had not married Steve. Vilma was overly concerned about Ida's reputation as a single woman while travelling the world without a commitment. For Ida it was not a priority to tie the knot mainly because she was still only 17 years old and not an overtly romantic and lovey-dovey type. Regardless, her mother kept insisting that she get married for another reason as well: Steve had fallen ill, and Vilma thought it was time for Ida to demonstrate her loyalty. Vilma thought that Steve was a good match for her daughter. The Gals knew his family and she believed that stemming from the same village was a strong bond that Ida could not find with someone else.

Serendipitously, during an appointment with the immigration services, Ida learned that if she wished to travel to America with her sweetheart, the only way the authorities would guarantee their entrance to the same country together was if they made it official. In addition, the only way they would continue placing them side by side was if they had the same last name. Ida being the logical person she is, now was ready to be wed. While the notion of matrimony didn't particularly appeal to her, she did want to stay with Steve and now necessity dictated their lifetime union.

Ida's maiden name started with a G, as in Gal, and Steve's last name started with a C as in Csiszar, so his paperwork was always processed before Ida's. Now Ida not only wished to marry Steve but wanted to take his last name which was much more commonly practiced then than it is today.

There were four other Hungarian couples who had similar challenges, so they were all trying to get to the altar. The town of Zierikzee came to the aid of the five couples and arranged a group wedding. Within a month of their arrival to the Netherlands, Ida and Steve were preparing for their big day and the locals could not have been any more generous!

A luminous and ivory bridal gown was loaned to her by the wife of an affluent doctor and Steve received his borrowed tuxedo by a successful businessman. If the outfits were beautiful, the ceremony was even more so! The best man was none other than a well-respected volunteer: the mayor of the city!

The biggest surprise was the source of their gold wedding bands. The Queen of the Netherlands, Juliana, herself gifted all of the couples their rings. Her daughter, Beatrix of the Netherlands, who was only a year older than Ida, delivered them to the ceremony on March 27, 1957. She flew in on a helicopter and handed the engraved rings to Ida and Steve, personally. The beaming bride, who was not familiar with royal protocol, hugged the alabaster-skinned princess who graciously received the embrace with a friendly smile. Needless to say, the press and media photographers were everywhere, and their group wedding picture was highlighted in the Dutch newspapers.

Now they were ready to depart the Netherlands hand-in-hand but still didn't know exactly to where they were advancing. The U.S. rejected Ida's and Steve's request because the country disallowed all patients with lung-related illnesses. Being in close proximity enough, Ida picked Canada instead. The first 200 Hungarian refugees were selected to cross the ocean on a luxury ship, yet again generously paid for by the Dutch. Ida felt extremely fortunate to have been chosen to make the big trip on such an upscale ocean liner with room service and full amenities. Not all émigrés got so lucky. The rest of them were put on a simple ship, named Ascania, and many of them crossed the Atlantic sleeping on the floor of the boat. Compared to them, Ida and Steve got the royal treatment—now, twice in a row!

Before they departed, the local stores opened their doors to those lucky 200 immigrants and donated high-quality clothes to them. Not one or two outfits but plenty to take with them to Canada. Shop owners encouraged the refugees to take whatever they felt they needed. The boutiques made sure the travelers had enough not only for the Spring but for all of the seasons. During their shopping spree they were allowed to choose any type of clothing from casual wear to upscale outfits and expensive gowns. There was no limit to the kindness and altruism of the locals. At the end, everyone received two suitcases full of superb clothing. As a result, the refugees ended up travelling to the New World looking like a million dollars. Getting on the Holland American Line on May 29, no one guessed that they were simple, poor asylum seekers.

Being well-dressed had always been important to both, Ida and Steve. Over time it became obvious to Ida that her initial thought about Steve, that he was vain, was far from the truth. The down to earth man's public image was far worse than who he really was. He was simply habitually chic just like Ida was; it was a habit they both kept all their lives. Being poor never prevented them from looking fashionable and elegant. They never ever bought junk but rather saved up their pennies for a few upscale pieces. "Quality over quantity." was their motto, even if it came from second-hand or thrift shops. If Steve saw a dress in a shop window that he though would look fabulous on Ida, he didn't hesitate to purchase it for her.

FULFILLING MY
AMERCIAN DREAM!

While at sea, Ida enjoyed the splendid treatment that came with travelling on a luxury ship. If she felt like wearing something fine to dinner she did, and if she preferred to stay in, she enjoyed being served in her cabin. She was now far from eating sausages out of a brief case at a crumbling railway station in Communist Hungary.

Because Steve was fighting TB, along with other patients, he was placed in the medical section of the ship. He too received the best hospitality and top-quality care that a country man from a quaint village in Eastern Europe could never have imagined.

Even though they were now husband and wife—they got married only two days before their departure—the authorities didn't have sufficient time to issue new documents for the now Mrs. Csiszar. Therefore, she left the Old World as a Gal and arrive to the New World in the same fashion.

CHAPTER FIVE

Silver Shimmer: The Country of Sequin

(Canada: June, 1957 – 1961)

5. <u>Canada: June, 1957 – 1961</u>

On the ocean liner Ida saw another Hungarian woman, Csibi, whose husband also had tuberculosis. Ida initially met her at the sanatorium in Holland and given their similar circumstances, they formed a friendship.

After a few days of sailing, they finally arrived in Halifax, Nova Scotia, Canada in June 1957. Once the ship pulled into the harbor, the first people who were released were the ones who needed medical attention. Steve and Csibi's husband were among them.

Ida saw them only from a distance because, due to safety concerns, she was not allowed to get too close. Witnessing their husbands being put on a bus, Ida and Csibi got nervous because the authorities hadn't informed the patients' relatives where they were taking them. Ida started to speed down the stairs, trying to get closer but a security guard attempted to stop her by grabbing her coat. That didn't faze her. She slipped out of the jacket and kept running all the way to the gate that separated the sick people from the rest of the passengers. She was still too far from Steve to talk to him but at least she could ask an officer what their plan was. Unfortunately, he didn't know much either and could not provide any information; nevertheless, he assured Ida that eventually she'd be informed and that they would be reunited.

Ida kept inquiring about Steve's whereabouts to anyone who would listen. Finally, she was told that all of the patients would be taken directly to a sanatorium, while the rest of the émigrés were transported to a refugee camp via locomotive. Where the sanatorium was exactly, no one seemed to know. Fortunately, all of the ship's passengers were put on the same train including the ill. At the beginning, Ida didn't know where Steve was, but she then heard that the very last compartment was dedicated to the sick separating them from the rest of the population. Ida was traveling in the front but wanted to check on Steve to ensure that he was all right.

Since visitation was not allowed, it was a real challenge to get to him. On top of it, the second to the last compartment presented itself to be a physical challenge: it was an actual kitchen complete with an ever-moving, busy cook. There was no way Ida could sneak over without being noticed but, she has never been the type to just give up and take no for an answer. She was committed to determining how possibly she could tip-toe across the bustling and aromatic kitchen. Eventually the opportunity presented itself: after keeping an eye on the cook for hours, at last she lifted the oversize lid off of the gigantic pot that had gallons of water boiling in it. That created so much steam around the stove that the cook didn't notice when Ida and Csibi snuck behind her back and crossed right over to the hospital section.

Soon after their unusual reunion with their dear husbands, the last car was disconnected from the train, the patients were transported to a bus and taken to a sanatorium while the train continued to its destination. Eventually, the wives were dropped off at the refugee camp in St. John, New Brunswick, where they would spend their first night in Canada. This place was specifically dedicated to families and children who had ill family members at a local medical facility.

Within hours Ida got to know other immigrants at the camp who told her where the sanatorium was: Moncton, New Brunswick. It was a few hours of hitchhiking away if she got lucky enough to be picked up quickly. The only issue was that Ida didn't know what hitchhiking was… Back in Gyoma, people didn't have cars, only tractors, horses, mules, scooters, and trains; she'd never heard of the word or seen how it was done. Her countrymen who had been in Canada for awhile had to explain to her which finger to use, how to hold her thumb up, and which side of the road to stand on. Ida was amazed at the concept that in the West all you had to do is situate yourself next to a turnpike and eventually someone gave you a ride to wherever you wanted to go.

After having completed the fresh immigrant's crash course of hitchhiking 101, she felt encouraged and was ready to put her newly acquired knowledge to the test. While today no reasonable person would hitchhike in North America, during that era it was an acceptable and safe way to move around if one was on a budget. After proposing this option to Csibi, they decided to pay a visit their husbands the next morning. They had no cash on them but that wasn't a problem for Ida. She was used to having nothing and still making things work.

Fellow immigrants mapped out how to get to Moncton. First Ida and Csibi had to get on a bus to take them to the highway. When the conductor came and asked for proof of purchase of the tickets, they were embarrassed to admit that they couldn't afford to buy them. With her basic knowledge of the language, Ida explained that they were Hungarians and had arrived in the country less then

FULFILLING MY AMERCIAN DREAM!

24 hours ago. The man was kind enough to let them ride all the way to the freeway for free, and fortuitously no passenger complained about him making an exception.

Once they arrived at their destination, everyone got off the bus except for them because they didn't realize the bus would not go any further. Once again, the conductor approached them, and they told him that they were going to hitchhike but being new to the area they didn't know how to reach the highway. It was at least a mile away and was not visible from the station. So, he drew a map, but it was not something they could comprehend. He then offered to give them a private ride on a public vehicle to the turnpike, and even walked them to the spot where they needed to stand.

They were picked up by the third car that approached. It was a sleek, convertible sports automobile with the top down; not something either of them had ever seen before. The couple in it was friendly and curious. The man behind the wheel asked where they were headed. Ida was grateful that he agreed to take them at least up to a certain point. Once they got comfortable, the four of them started to converse. Ida spoke a little bit of English that she had learned from her aunt, in addition to studying on her own while in Austria and the Netherlands.

It didn't take long for the duo to find out where Ida and Csibi were from. By this time many Canadians had heard of Hungary's heroic freedom fight and the consequential mass migration after the Soviets crushed it. From the onset, this North American country was one of the most welcoming ones to Hungarians; it was rumored that for a while it accepted the greatest number of immigrants. Once the couple found out about their trials and tribulations and why they were going to the sanatorium, the driver changed his mind and offered to take them all the way to the hospital.

Around noon, the owner of the car decided to stop at a restaurant near a gas station for lunch. He pulled over and asked Ida and Csibi whether they were hungry. Yes, they were! The driver asked his partner to take the women to eat. As all the ladies were heading toward the deli's entrance, Ida asked why he wasn't joining them. "Because he has no legs." the girlfriend said. Apparently, the convertible was solely maneuvered manually and, while sitting in it, Ida didn't realize that his lower limbs were completely missing. After they ordered their lunch, they brought him a warm entrée, he ate it in the vehicle, and then they continued their journey. The man shared that he was a journalist and Ida speculated that for the rest of the trip he was gathering information for a piece.

The spacious and busy medical facility's address was in the city of Moncton, but the actual building was outside the city. Both husbands were surprised and amazed to hear how their wives conquered the big distance and came to see them. As time went on, Ida and Csibi regularly traveled between the refugee camp and the sanatorium, paying their husbands visits. When occasionally she couldn't go, Ida and Steve corresponded with each other via postal mail. Ida and Csibi went back and forth so many times that eventually the hospital allowed them to stay overnight. One of the sections of the building was closed to medical services, but had

beds in it, so the welcoming staff here and there allowed them to

spend the night. Not only that, but the extended hospitality

included surplus meals that had not been served to the patients.

The beautiful mountains and forests surrounding the clinic were so

enchanting, Ida loved taking long walks in the area enjoying its

fresh air and gorgeous fauna.

While waiting for Steve to recover from tuberculosis, Ida took a

job as a housekeeper with a family who had three children. She

worked Monday through Friday and her duties included cleaning,

taking care of the laundry, and being the nanny to the kids whose

parents were serious alcoholics. Many a time it was Ida who

needed to distract the youngsters from their own parents'

addiction. Frequently, the only respite she found was taking them

upstairs and not letting the toddlers witness their parents being out

of control.

FULFILLING MY AMERCIAN DREAM!

Even though it was mentally draining, she enjoyed the challenging position. However, ultimately her visits with her spouse became regular weekend stays, and after a while Ida decided to relocate and be nearby Steve.

The government's assistance program also found it to be a clever idea for her to move to Moncton and find a rentable room there. Ida told the social worker that she wanted to find a job and make money, but they paid for the temporary lease, along with her basic expenses, so she was able to assist Steve instead.

After relocating, Ida met a fellow Hungarian, named Kalman. The middle-aged expat, who, to the teenaged Ida seemed ancient, was a mechanic. He also was in the infirmary but was released six months before Steve. Kalman stayed in the area and worked at a local gas station to save enough money to buy a vehicle. He proposed to Ida that when her husband got released, they, along with another couple who were spending time in the medical facility, could drive to Toronto together and leave Moncton behind. While they were waiting for Steve's discharge, Kalman had plenty of time to get his newly-bought used vehicle fixed up for the trip.

While overall life at the time was uneventful, something very special happened that would affect Ida's and Steve's lives forever. Ida got pregnant with their first child. She told the joyous news to Steve but otherwise kept it a secret because she didn't want to risk her travel companions changing their minds about taking them to Toronto.

When they were ready for the journey, Kalman cooked up a storm for the road. He made pork chops, brought sausages, and he baked Hungarian dishes; the vehicle smelled deliciously like an ethnic café. Now they were indeed ready to take off for the largest city in the country. Maxing out the vehicle's capacity and equally sharing all the expenses allowed them to minimize the costs. The reason they decided on Toronto was rather trivial: one of them had a relative there and since Moncton didn't have much to offer, they figured a metropolis was a better choice.

While Kalman was driving, Ida navigated based on the foldout maps. Eventually, they had to get some sleep so they chose the least expensive motel they could find. The clerk suggested three rooms when Ida explained to her that the five of them only wanted one. She assured them that was not possible given no suite had enough beds for all of them. It wasn't beds they needed though but a roof over their heads—Ida responded. They were willing to sleep on the floor since that's all they could afford. Renting one was better than renting none, the cheap motel's receptionist thought, and they struck a deal.

After getting settled in the room, Kalman took the vehicle to the mechanic shop to ensure everything was running smoothly. Unfortunately, something was wrong with the car and it took him all night to fix it. By chance, the friendly owner of the auto repair allowed Kalman to do all the work that was necessary for no charge so they could continue driving.

The next morning, Steve told Ida that he was going to hitchhike over to the shop to see how the transportation situation was coming along; but no one would pick him up. Ida came to his rescue and told him to go home and let her handle it like a pro. Given what an attractive woman she was the very first car—which happened to be an American one—

stopped. The driver struck up a conversation, asked where she was from, what she was doing in the area, and how she landed in Canada. Ida felt compelled to share her entire story and why she was there instead of America, even though the U.S.A is where she wanted to live all of her life. It was heartbreaking that Steve could not get a visa to the U.S. due to his history of tuberculosis and that Ida couldn't be with her sister—her only close relative —who by that time lived in nearby Philadelphia. Ida and Irene missed each other very much especially now that they were both pregnant! Even though the siblings were on the same continent they had not seen each other in quite awhile. Still speaking with imperfect English, Ida wondered whether she understood the man correctly when he said that he was a politician and a U.S. senator. He pointed into the distance and showed her roughly where the border was and asked whether she would move there if he made it possible for them. Ida didn't quite fathom how he would be able to assist them with overcoming their significant administrative and legal obstacles, but he just kept repeating for her not to worry about it. He, in fact, would be able to take care of it all. Barely a legal adult, Ida was not grasping how official matters could be turned around with such efficiency, so she didn't truly consider accepting the too-good-to-be-true offer. In the back of her mind, she was afraid of accidentally not following the law, being caught, and then being dragged back to Hungary. She knew that if they returned there and the Communists had authority over them again, that could be the end of it. She very well knew that Steve was a wanted man in Hungary not only for escaping the country, but for deserting the army. The senator seemed to understand that particular matter well given that he had knowledge about international affairs and that may have been the reason he tried to reassure her. What she related to him did not appear to be problematic from his point of view. Perhaps because their interaction happened just a few years after the American Communist Control Act had passed and McCarthyism was still around. The senator reiterated that he'd be able to take care of their immigration affairs, but she was concerned about the authenticity of his words. What if he could not take care of all the necessary paperwork and they ended up being deported? Exaggerated fears or not, she didn't want to risk what she already had so far. While his words sounded credible and convincing, she didn't know him well enough to make such an enormous change solely based on a one-time conversation. So, she thanked him and got out of the vehicle at the gas station's service center.

Kalman finally fixed the car and they were elated to be able to get back on the road. Driving through French Canada, they couldn't resist stopping in Quebec and getting their hands on the most tasty,

FULFILLING MY AMERCIAN DREAM!

doughy, and fresh bread just out of the oven to go with the last servings of their five-star leftover meals.

Upon arriving at Toronto's immigration office, they learned something that they didn't know before. The officers were waiting for them with open arms. Not only because they wanted to assist them, but because they were urgently looking for people to work on ranches. Already established Hungarian expats were also eager to offer their fellow country(wo)men jobs. Simply put they were in demand!

Her husband's health history was weighing heavily on Ida's mind; she was afraid that they would not get hired anywhere. Seeing no other option, she accepted an offer to work on a tobacco field. The given plantation was owned by a compassionate and highly intellectual Hungarian Jewish couple, Dr. & Mrs. Sampson. Along with two other Magyar couples, Ida and Steve moved to the designated agricultural area in hopes of sorting out their immigration status later.

FULFILLING MY AMERCIAN DREAM!

Right across the field, they received a little shack to live in that even had electricity, which was a luxury in a rural environment. All the same, it didn't have an indoor bathroom only an outdoor one. Nevertheless, Ida thought it was a pleasant place and most importantly they had roof over their heads. They furnished it modestly from the local Salvation Army store where the owners took them shopping. Since they were refugees, they received all the items for free: a mattress, two tables, and everything else that was necessary to create a home and to prepare for the eventual arrival of their child.

Dr. and Mrs. Sampson were very sympathetic to Ida's situation. Having survived both the Holocaust and the Soviet Gulag themselves; they understood the risks Ida had to take to get out of her Hungary. They were beyond supportive when they learned that Ida was pregnant: they offered to take her to her doctor visits and assisted with whatever else Ida needed.

Nearby there was another enterprise; its business was wood instead of tobacco, and that's where Steve got a job. First, he had to chop up the pieces and then make pallets out of them by nailing the parts together. While he was doing that, Ida was handling the fresh tobacco plants as it was now springtime. First, she needed to pull the healthy baby bushes from the greenhouse and then put them in the ground for growing. The owner sat on a tractor and drove it forward while Ida placed the individual seedlings in the machine that was attached to the tractor. Then the machine pushed them into the soil. Later on, Ida had to hoe around the growing shrubs, which she did while carrying her baby to term and dealing with swollen legs caused by her arteries. In the fall, once they had broken off the ripe, tobacco leaves, they had to hang them indoors to dry them thoroughly. The manual labor was broken into sub-tasks so that the process would be fluid and fast. Ida's job was to hand another worker the green foliage so that said worker could tie them together, climb up a ladder, and hang them high on the ceiling in the warehouse.

FULFILLING MY AMERCIAN DREAM!

In the midst of all the physical labor, on November 21, 1958, their first son, Steven, was born in Alliston, Simcoe County. It was just a month after the birth of Irene's son, John Jr. The owners of the plantation took Ida to the hospital, notified Steve, then the couple patiently waited for her to give birth in the delivery room.

Instantaneously, everyone fell in love with the baby, so the elderly couple was delighted to keep an eye on Steven and teach Ida the ins and outs of motherhood. Since Ida couldn't afford to hire a babysitter, Mrs. Sampson invited her to bring her infant with her to work so Steven would always be supervised. Ida wouldn't have left Steven alone anyway but allowing her to leave him inside the boss' home and feed him when he got hungry was especially helpful. Dr. and Mrs. Sampson's selflessness left a lifetime imprint on Ida and she cherished their friendship for years to come.

By the time winter came around, all the moisture had evaporated from the brown leaves and Ida now needed to take each three-piece bunch apart. While still working on the farm, the new parents found a more spacious house, owned by an elderly couple, in the village. They welcomed them with open arms and Csiszars moved off the plantation. Their new place was simple too. It had a bedroom, a kitchen, and a wooden stove, and that was about it. At their new location, Steve met a man from whom he learned that there was a better-paying job available on the army base: large barracks were being disassembled. His new friend put in a good word for Steve and he got the job!

Their salaries were not remarkable, but enough that they were able to put money aside to buy a car, although neither of them could drive. They had to hastily learn if they wanted to make their lives easier. The automobile was nothing fancy, but dependable enough that it allowed Steve to drop Ida off in the morning, commute to his work, and pick her up at the end of the day.

Even though the countryside in Ontario was beautiful, Ida didn't want to stay indefinitely. After a year, she wanted to move to Toronto where they rented the upstairs level of a house. At the beginning, they had to work really hard to survive in the metropolis.

Having had experience as a medic, Steve was immediately able to land a job as a night nurse in an emergency room saving lives, while Ida started to work in a different department in the same hospital; she assisted in the kitchen. First, they only let her do the dishes, then she collected the dirty plates from the dining hall and put out the clean ones when it was time. It wasn't long before her supervisors realized that she was way too clever and ambitious, and they could trust her with making more responsible decisions. Based on strict nutritional guidelines she was now asked to place the patients' food on their trays before mealtime. While this sounded like a simple task, it was far from it. Every single patient's case needed to be reviewed daily and accordingly she made dietary decisions. She was trained in food distribution for people with diabetes and other special needs and as a dietitian's aid, her hourly rate went up. Though Ida and Steve each worked only one shift a day, they alternated their hours because someone needed to be with their Steven.

Focusing on having enough to live on as much as expanding their clan, Ida and Steve agreed on having a second child. Accordingly, she now needed an even better paying position, so she got a similar job at an upscale veteran's club. It catered to wounded, high-ranking officers lacking limbs or challenged by other substantial health conditions.

The aristocratic building that housed the military association was nothing short of an exclusive museum. It was full of valuable oil paintings and sculptures depicting World War I & II and, according to Ida, it was the most opulent place where she has ever worked.

There she had to wear a white uniform with a white cap, white gloves, and a black apron for lunch and a black uniform with a black cap, black gloves, and a white apron for dinner. She served the disabled and the sick from 11 AM till 2 PM and then she went back for supper at 5 PM. She learned elite table etiquette: how to serve certain dishes, what way to set the table properly and the utensils for multiple courses, and from which side of the diner she needed to approach them. Before the patients even sat down to the table, she needed to assure that their glasses were immaculately clean and polished. She then took their orders, passed them on to the kitchen, and then delivered their meals on a cart.

She was now earning so much more money than she used to on the tobacco plantation. She got more in tips than her hourly wage and the additional benefit was that her free mornings and afternoons breaks allowed her to be at home with her tribe.

No matter how fantastic she felt her job was, by nature, was always on the lookout for something even better. According, she regularly scanned the newspaper's job section and one day she found an ad that really interested her artistically as well as financially.

FULFILLING MY AMERCIAN DREAM!

A film studio, named Kodak—that made documentaries and educational shorts—and focused on editing and film restoration—was looking for film cutters. Ida didn't know anything about editing, production, post-production, or restoration, but she applied anyway and surprisingly got hired as an assistant whose task was to preselect footage.

The company trained Ida for the chronological steps of the work flow: each cinematographer had his assigned editor, and occasionally a senior cameraman would have two. Once the shooters brought in their footage, in collaboration with a footage selector, they would assemble the moving images. Ida was three times as fast as the rest of the aids so within months the management inquired whether she was interested in being promoted to create cine-montages herself.

Her initial step was to take a crash course in movie making. She found the entire process fascinating and creatively satisfying. She was now in charge and if she deemed it necessary, Ida had the right to request the photo journalist to do retakes.

At Kodak, she was on the job by 8 AM while Steve worked nights; this way they could avoid hiring a babysitter. While this schedule was taxing on the pair's intimate life, it served the needs of their son, so they stuck with it until Steve got sick again. A growing tumor appeared on his forehead, developed from a sinus infection and he needed to have an operation. Though it was not cancerous, it was right above his eye and interfered with his vision. They had to cut open not only his tumor but his eye below and Ida became quite worried. Irene and John suggested that they relocate to the U.S. so they could give a hand and finally be together as a family during another challenging phase of their lives.

While Steve didn't, Ida had a Canadian green card already, but that didn't allow her to stay in America longer than six months. In the midst of all this, Kodak decided to move to a new location in San Francisco, California. Due to Ida's high level of productivity and charming personality, they liked her very much, so her supervisor invited her to come along. While she was very interested in the Bay Area, Ida already had her eyes set on New Brunswick, New Jersey, USA because that's where her sister and brother-in-law lived. Her boss pleaded with Ida to move with them to the West Coast, so he asked her to reconsider and even gave her his private number. He wanted to have her on staff so badly, he made her promise that if she ever changed her mind, she'd ring him, and he'd take her back. However, Ida was willing to give up a genuinely interesting and promising career with an excellent salary, to be near her loved ones instead. After seven years in Canada and four years in Toronto, Ida was ready for the next chapter and was actively waiting for the stars to align.

Shortly afterwards she found out that she was pregnant with their second child. That was the good news. The bad news was that her issues with her arteries from her first pregnancy resurfaced and the situation was getting increasingly alarming. She needed to have an operation but could not find a Canadian doctor to go through with the procedure for the very reason that she was expecting. Ida was hoping to carry her baby full term, but her arteries were getting so compromised that she could hardly walk. She needed urgent intervention.

Irene was concerned about Ida's state, so she had a discussion with her Hungarian American physician who assisted with her son's birth. While today most medical professionals are highly specialized, back in those days the spectrum of general doctors was much wider. After carefully examining the facts, he told Irene to press Ida to come to the U.S. and he would take care of her veins, but on the condition that after the operation, he would deliver the baby himself. The physician had to keep an eye on the expectant mother for the remainder of the pregnancy and during her labor to assure everything went smoothly.

Due to visa issues, Ida grabbed her toddler, left Steve behind in Canada, and headed to New Brunswick, NJ. The M.D. operated on her when she was four months pregnant and luckily, everything went smoothly without any problems. Ida's leg healed up impeccably and five months later, in 1961, Frank was born on U.S. soil. Now her infant was an American citizen, but it was illegal for her to stay any longer, so she packed her bags and children, and went back to Toronto.

In Canada, Ida couldn't stop thinking about reuniting with Irene's family. After some time and much consideration, they decided to take a chance, cross the U.S. border and attempt to sort out their American immigration issues in New Jersey.

CHAPTER SIX

The Coast of Cream Satin

(USA – East Coast: 1961–1973)

6. <u>USA – East Coast: 1961 – 1973</u>

"Staying over" didn't prove to be a successful strategy even though at first Ida was granted an extensive stay. It may sound naïve, but hopelessly wanting to be legal, Ida even physically sent Steve to the White House to ask the first man there for a permanent resident status. Of course, every American knows that the Immigration and Naturalization Service, commonly known as the INS—not the White House—is the one that handles immigration requests. Accordingly, Steve's knocking on the President's door resulted in a smirk on the FBI agent's face but not a green card.

Ida desperately tried to find someone, anyone who would listen and understand that she needed to be close to her sister since she had two children to feed and her husband was not a particularly healthy man. Ida quickly learned what any foreigner knows that in general immigrating to the United States is an unfairly complicated, taxingly expensive, and dishearteningly time-consuming process.

Ida and Steve spent all their hard-earned money on finding appropriate and legal means to stay in the U.S.A., but nobody was able to ease their troubles. After two years of this futility, she became panic-stricken. She could not stop ruminating about the possibility of being deported and sent back to Communism. She especially got anxious after John F. Kennedy's assassination and one day, in the beginning of 1964, she just had enough! In an act of despair, she decided to write to none other but the new President of the United States. In her letter, she introduced herself to Lyndon B. Johnson and told him her entire story. She stated the reason of her wanting to stay in the country, and at the bottom of her correspondence, respectfully requested his assistance.

FULFILLING MY AMERCIAN DREAM!

Astonishingly, about a week later, she got a one-page response signed by no other than President Johnson himself! He instructed her to get to the nearest immigration office and promised Ida that "you'll be taken care of."

Ida and Steve arrived at the federal building and without showing the communiqué from the White House, she told their names to the officer. She stated that they were from Canada and that they have come to legalize their status. The condescending agent responded that they needed to "return to the land of Canooks immediately", otherwise he would start their deportation right then and there.

In that very instant, Ida pulled from her pocket her golden ticket to her future and shoved President Johnson's letter in the guard's face. As his jaw dropped, the man's expression was priceless! Stunned and stuttering he apologized, well, as much as a stuttering person can, and told them to follow him. He led them to an office with a desk that had their file on top, right in the center. The dossier was stamped with large, red letters: SPECIAL. The folder not only contained their paperwork of legalization but the commander in chief's letter as well. Within minutes, they were each granted a visa, three years later Ida and Steve got their green cards, and in five years, on exactly the same day of their visit to the INS, they became citizens of the United States of America. After years of uncertainty and distress, Ida's childhood dream came true at last and finally she felt she was in paradise! In her eyes, everything in America was made of gold or at least everything could be turned into gold.

Now as a resident, she visited New York and when she laid eyes on the Empire State Building—just like her aunt years before—she couldn't stop sobbing. Ida knew of many immigrants who had identical reactions when arriving to the Big Apple, possibly because their backgrounds and sensibilities were similar. However, in her mind where you came from mattered not. What did matter was what was going to happen after they got settled—what they were going to do with their lives when finally given the right opportunities. What mattered was what they were going to show for the years and decades that they were going to spend in the U.S., and what they were going to accomplish with their blood, sweat, and tears. After all, now each one of them had the chance to make something of themselves, and Ida was determined to be one of those who would become a somebody!

As most somebodies, she also started at the bottom. First, she managed an apartment building while Steve held a position at a gas station. As industrious as Ida was, it didn't take long before she found a job that would become not just the foundation of her business, but her life as well. For her, landing a managerial position in the baby department's quality control division with Johnson & Johnson was like winning the lottery!

From the beginning, Ida felt at home at Johnson & Johnson even though it was enormous; the building she worked in had approximately 4,000 employees. While no official data are available, to Ida it seemed that the corporation loved the Magyars. According to her, 70% of the laborers were from her country.

FULFILLING MY AMERCIAN DREAM!

There were rumors that Johnson & Johnson even sent large ships to Germany to transport Hungarian refugees so that they could employ them. True or not, it was a warm, welcoming, and amiable environment in which to work. If being surrounded by that many of her country(wo)men was not sufficient, Ida realized that in the neighboring city, Highland Park, even the mayor was her own ethnicity. Ida was far from her childhood home yet, in many ways, remained so close.

Her first assignments tied her closely to the assembly line where she saw a lot of room for improvement. At the time, Johnson & Johnson paid $20-$75 for every new idea that improved productivity and efficiency and Ida gave them plenty. Many of hers saved the company time on the assembly line; for instance, one such suggestion improved packaging techniques and the speed of folding and sealing shipping boxes. Make no mistake though, none of these concepts were revolutionary, but at the end of the day, many of her mini eureka moments ended up making a huge difference and saved a lot of money. While the compensation for her concepts felt rewarding, money was not the reason for her creative thinking. Instead, her observant nature allowed her to come up with all these suggestions easily. She had always enjoyed the challenge of finding ways to improve things. Perhaps even as an employee, consciously or unconsciously, she strived towards being inventive, able to think on her feet, becoming successful, and being the boss. While she has always paid attention to being clean and presentable, wearing shiny shoes, and having a stylish hairdo, at Johnson & Johnson she started to wear makeup and nail polish! She was slowly transforming herself into a leader and her inner changes manifested themselves externally.

She made many useful proposals while at Johnson & Johnson; one that she was especially known for was the so-called cotton ball concept. There were different types of bags thrown onto the conveyor belt and, based on size, at the end those needed to be sorted into three different boxes. Once those bins filled up, Ida needed to remove the content first, so the new packets transported on the conveyor belt could continue dropping in. Ida's suggestion was, that they order cases that had an opening at the bottom and instead of lifting each trunk every time it got full, they could just dump its content into a larger storage carton. This would allow speeding up not only the emptying of the squares but the motion of the production line.

When Ida presented her notion to Johnson & Johnson, they ordered the new type of boxes. When the bottom-opening bins were installed, those made such a difference in production that the management acted like Ida had invented the universe!

At Johnson & Johnson there were three available shifts for her department which she worked for ten years: 7 AM - 3 PM, 3 PM - 11 PM, 11 PM - 6 AM. Both, Ida's and Steve's work used the same schedule but each worked different shifts so the kids would have their own parents watching them at all times. If she worked the 3 AM -11 PM shift, he worked the 11 PM- 6 AM shift. The overlapping few minutes were covered by a neighbor's older son. The couple hardly saw each other, so their closeness began to suffer and cracks in the relationship started to appear. Fundamentally all they did was work and parent and there just wasn't enough time in the day time for romance. Their kids were their priority, so they did what a hard-working immigrant family had to do pull themselves up by their bootstraps, and play catch-up on the weekends, although many times they even had to work on Saturdays and Sundays.

Apparently, working all the time and raising two children wasn't enough of a challenge for Ida; she decided to go to college and study business and manufacturing. Johnson & Johnson had close ties to Rutgers University, so it was an obvious choice for her. She rushed to her classes straight from work, but quickly she realized that she couldn't fulfill all of her obligations all of the time. If her lecture happened to fall on a day when Ida and Steve were both off and he could watch the kids, she would definitely attend. However, when there was no one to attend to Steven and Frank, she had to skip it. Fortunately, given her company's relationship with the university, the professors were quite tolerant if she was not able to be present. She went to college on and off for years, but in the end, she could not complete enough units to earn a degree. Instead, she received a Certificate in Business Administration which later came in handy. While at Rutger's, she discovered that she absolutely loved science, especially chemistry relating to the beauty industry. However, she loathed the animal testing that was very common at the time, so she tried to find a way to circumvent.

In 1968, the first time since she fled her country, Ida finally had the opportunity to take a vacation and go back and visit her dearest family. She took both of her children to show them where their parents were from. They flew with a cross-continental flight to Vienna where her reserved car with automatic transmission was supposed to be waiting. Right after the long and tiresome flight, she had planned to drive to Hungary. Despite the reservation, when she landed with her exhausted kids, the rental company declared that they had run out of vehicles. Being worn out herself, Ida lost her patience and went ballistic, so much so, that the manager left no stone unturned to remedy the situation on an emergency basis.

FULFILLING MY AMERCIAN DREAM!

Unfortunately, the only car he could find had a stick shift which she didn't know how to drive. Being the only option, she requested a crash course right there at the airport while her youngsters stood by waiting for their mother to complete her driving lesson.

After crossing into Hungary, Ida instructed her sons to throw the Western cigarettes and chewing gum she brought out the window, so they would not be bothered by the soldiers. The trick did wonders, their journey continued until she needed to park…

During that era, Westerners were never difficult to spot in Hungary especially when they wore world class outfits and maroon lipstick. Also, it was a peculiar thing for a woman to drive an automobile without a man in it. Law enforcement spotted her and signaled her to stop and pull into their open garage. With some maneuvering she was able to slow down but parking with a stick was a different matter… When she finally came to a full stop, she told them that she had just learned to drive hours ago, so if they wanted her to be in *that* particular lot, they would need to push the car themselves.

FULFILLING MY AMERCIAN DREAM!

The authorities subjected Ida's luggage to a thorough search. Of course, Ida knew well in advance that it was going to happen, so all the luxurious and expensive gifts she brought for her relatives, were placed at the bottom of her suitcase. To avoid them getting confiscated, she put plenty of novelty items on the top of her clothing. She was certain that sex, alcohol, and sweets sell. Once the officers saw the Playboy magazines, bottles of whiskey, delicious chocolate, and colorful chewing gum covering Ida's used blouses, they didn't bother continuing their search. Trying to keep a straight face and attempting to sound serious and official, they informed her that all the indecent nude magazines and evil Jack Daniel's were illegal in the country. She could hardly wait for them to finish their sentences—shamefully looking down at the pavement—she apologized and asked whether they would be kind enough to throw those into the garbage can for her. They couldn't volunteer fast enough, and Ida was happy to continue her journey home.

FULFILLING MY AMERCIAN DREAM!

As you may imagine, Ida's go-getter personality influenced her cruising style as well—even if she didn't really know how to handle the wheel. Being behind schedule, she didn't hesitate to step on the gas and speeded like a free-spirited racecar driver across her slow and suppressed country. Just before leaving Austria, she phoned home and told everyone that she'd be there by three o'clock. Delivering on time as always, she rolled in front of their house in Gyoma at exactly 3:00 PM and couldn't stop hugging and kissing her crying parents and laughing siblings, who in the meantime had grown up. They loved having Ida back and couldn't have been any prouder of her.

Introducing her children to her relatives and spending a lot of time with her mother and father made Ida happy. On the other hand, Ida noticed that Hungary was nothing as she remembered it to be everything was dark, ugly, and subdued. Nevertheless, she wanted her kids to find the beauty in the land, so she purposefully brainwashed her sons by repeatedly telling them how gorgeous it was.

While she was there, feeling a bit guilty, she asked around to find out what ever happened to her would-be date from 1956, Sandor. It was no surprise that he too defected and was happily living in France. Ida also wondered whether the official they met at Mezotur's railway station while eating spicy sausages had ever told on them, especially when it became widespread that Ida and Steve defected. She made multiple inquiries, but no one really knew for certain.

While in Gyoma, it was worrisome that the secret police were spying on Ida the entire time she was there. The AVO still wished to get their hands-on Steve, but he was smart enough to stay behind. They were trying to gather as much information on her husband as they could, but Ida knew what she was doing and when she returned to America, she made sure to leave them behind wanting more.

Per local regulations, upon departing, she was supposed to check in with the police in Gyoma and pick up a so-called "departure slip" and then hand it to the authorities once she got to the border. This was a mandatory document used by the guards to green light her to exit from Hungary. Upon saying her good byes to Vilma and Ferenc, Ida got into her car without recalling having to attend to this; after all, who remembers that sort of bureaucratic nonsense? Hundreds of miles later when she got to Austria, she was faced with a nerve-racking situation: the police were not allowing her to leave and threatening Ida to keep her hostage. It took all her negotiating skills, charm, and some bribing so that the officers would not keep her in a country that now represented her past and instead open the gate for her to the free world.

This wasn't the only time Ida felt her guardian angels protected her on her journey. Once back in the U.S, Steve was in the hospital again, and her station wagon broke down in the dark, snowy, icy weather. She spotted a phone booth at a gas station, but she had no change on her to make an emergency call. Standing there, not knowing what to do, without touching the telephone, suddenly 20 pieces of change fell out of the coin slots with which she was able to dial the number for roadside assistance and get home safely. While some may say this was just a coincidence, in Ida's life these serendipitous events occurred too frequently for her not to give meaning to them.

Having gotten settled back in her American life, she received news she'd been waiting for years. The government of Hungary finally allowed Ida's parents to visit her. They were the first wave of individuals who were permitted to get a passport and travel abroad. In a democracy, people take it for granted that one can obtain a passport anytime because in a free society it's not a privilege but a right. On the other hand, in a dictatorship it's the opposite. For years, Hungarians were not guaranteed to be able to take trips. Depending on how oppressive the regime wished to be, people needed to get different permits to move around. There were three distinct levels of authorizations: domestic, foreign travel to Communist countries, and trips to Western countries. Since so many citizens never returned from their Western trips, the government made it nearly impossible to fly to America. Usually, the government only granted authorization to old, disabled, or relatively well-off citizens since it was less likely for them to defect Hungary. Ida's parents waited for theirs for years but at last they were approved. For Ida this was an extremely important moment. Somehow, her parents never truly comprehended why she always wanted to come to America: how this country was better than Hungary and what type of opportunities existed.

Once they landed and had the chance to look around Ida's chosen land, they finally understood, and most importantly, approved of her decision. The feeling that she surpassed her parents' expectations gave Ida wings. It was especially significant because she had wanted to be in the financial position to be generous with her parents, make their lives easier, and provide support to her siblings who had stayed behind. From then on, now that they had money, Ida and Steve invited both of their parents to the U.S.

frequently and did everything in their power to make their families' lives better and richer.

Since Ida and Steve had always stayed close to their roots and attempted to carry on with their culture as well as their families' traditions, creating a magical Christmas was a top priority. One year, when Steve could not earn any money because he was hospitalized repeatedly, he requested to be released on Christmas Eve to spend the holiday with his family. After picking him up and taking him home to be with the kids, Ida went Christmas tree shopping. She was still getting used to the cultural difference in the timing of trimming the tree. Back in the Old World, due to plenty of winter festivities starting in November—such as Advent, St. Nicholas Day on December 6, and St. Lucy's Day on December 13—as opposed to Americans, who traditionally start preparing the day after Thanksgiving, Hungarians only decorate their trees on Christmas Eve. Therefore, it is not uncommon for them to purchase a tree on the day of. By the time Ida got to the lot, there was only one humongous, 11-foot tall tree left. It was obvious that she was not going to be able to fit it into her car, so she asked the salesman to cut it in half, but he refused. She then requested that the tree be tied to the top of her car, making the transport easier because of the thick rope. This also meant, she had to roll down the windows somewhat and drive like that in the winter. Trying to position it correctly, the poor tree was still hanging off the back, but Ida with her feisty spirit didn't let that interfere. She was going to get her kids a tree, even if she had to maneuver that drive for ten miles. Added to the challenge, it started to seriously snow, and visibility became close to non-existent. Slowly, but surely, she finally made it home safely with a tree that had frozen needles. She was now ready to saw the tree in half herself and while she cooked a festive dinner, she let her sons trim the hard-earned Christmas tree under which she later smuggled everyone's gifts.

As time went by, instead of working at the factory, Ida thought it would be better for Steve to open his own "mom and pop" type business. He would deliver food supplies with his truck that they had bought for this specific purpose. There was a warehouse where they could purchase various items at a discounted rate and then cargo them to smaller grocery stores. The center provided Steve with the locations of the shops that were interested in receiving fresh produce. Steve worked hard for his profit. He needed to get up at 4 AM every day to distribute the packages. Once his vehicle was empty, he then had to drive back to the distributor in the afternoon, fill it up with merchandise, and then in the morning start all over again. He was usually able to deliver all of the packages by 2-3 PM in the afternoon since the stores placed orders in advance and he always knew what to pick up for each outlet. Steve made relatively good money with his service, cash flow was continuous, and he was satisfied.

Once this business was running smoothly, Ida came up with yet another business concept. But, in order for Steve to start focusing on his wife's brainchild, they first had to hire someone to drive the delivery truck. Many of the veterans who returned from Vietnam were putting themselves out in the job market and Ida and Steve hired one of them. Steve conscientiously trained the new guy, showed him all the stores, how to do the pick-ups and drop-offs, and how to properly load. Sadly, the subcontracting didn't go as well as they originally hoped. Three days after their new employee started the job, the police showed up at Ida's house informing her that they found an abandoned and burnt vehicle in the mountains that was registered under their name. Apparently, the fellow they had hired didn't pay attention, lost control, and the vehicle went up in flames. Ida and Steve never saw the man again; he never bothered to give them the time of the day and explain what happened. To make the news even worse, because Ida and Steve didn't have any insurance, they had to absorb the loss. Losing the van also meant losing enterprise. That was all right with Ida though because in her mind she was already onto something more profitable: general contracting.

Just days before, Ida had a discussion with Paul, the Hungarian Mayor with whom she was recently acquainted. He had asked whether Ida knew any workers who would be able to repair roofs, paint walls, and fix up buildings, and that's how Ida had an "aha moment". He added that there would be an abundance of orders since the City Hall needed to be renovated and it was hard to find good contractors those days.

While she was starting their new business, Ida and Steve heard that more people were escaping Hungary and many of them were heading to New York. Their first thought was: to help them so they can establish themselves in America quickly! A long time ago they promised themselves that if they could ever come to their fellow countrymen's aid, they would—the same way they were assisted. Steve went to the city and at the immigration office tried to find newcomers to offer them free lodging and food, and decent-paying jobs so they could get on their feet as soon as possible. By this time the couple had a four-bedroom house with a recreation room, and a cellar, so they had plenty of space to provide comfort and hospitality. Steve chose three Hungarian men and, as luck would have it, a few days later Ida found out that they had experience with roofing, plumbing, and painting: she immediately put two and two together and realized they were able to offer the Hungarian refugees work.

By this time, they already had a dedicated telephone line for their new business, and an advertisement campaign in place, so the phone started ringing off the hook. Ida learned that the local Chief of Police was also Hungarian, so she phoned him and asked for additional referrals. In a short amount of time, their business grew exponentially and expanded beyond residential buildings. Once the contracts for commercial buildings, churches, and city-owned property were in place, their business thrived, and they wanted their employees to benefit from it as well.

However, Ida's challenges started growing out of proportion. The refugees were not as reliable as she needed them to be. Sometimes they showed up for work and sometimes they disappeared and that worried Ida a lot. In addition, it was Ida, not Steve, who was the one who increasingly had to carry the load of their mutual business in addition to raising two children, having a full-time job, and keeping the household running. Steve had become discouraged and Ida wasn't sure how she could possibly handle any more. Her partner in life who was supposed to be her partner in business, frequently asked Ida to run to the store and get materials for their construction sites such as nails, screws, paint, and insulation. During her lunch breaks at Johnson & Johnson, she ran to get the men everything they requested and then rushed back to work. If she was lucky, she had a few minutes to grab a couple of bites to eat. For all intents and purposes, Ida was becoming the laborers' assistant which didn't particularly set well with her. Due to the pressure of juggling so many aspects of their lives, Ida was becoming mentally and physically exhausted, and routinely taking care of Steve and his employees was becoming too much.

One day when she had to deliver the materials to the men yet again, she saw something she couldn't believe. All of them, including her husband, were sitting on the rooftop and instead of working non-stop like she was, they were lounging around and having beers. That was the straw that broke the camel's back. Ida became furious and after yelling at them, she turned around, went home, and announced that she was ready to leave him! She made it abundantly clear that she was not the sort of woman who runs around for a man, so he can sit around drinking booze! Right then and there, she decided to sell the house and move to Southern California! Her sister now lived there, and Ida had a friend who was a real estate agent, so she reached out that day and told her to sell the house including all the furniture and the knick-knacks.

At first Steve didn't give credence to it but then it started to dawn on him that maybe she did mean it after all… Ida told him that she had had enough and that she was going to Los Angeles. Their house sold in three days and within a week everything else was gone as well, including their beautiful 1965 Chevy Impala.

Meanwhile, she confined in a friend of hers who happened to be a divorce lawyer. She told her that she could not go on with the way things were, but at the end of the day she didn't really want to break up their union. However, if she did consider separating in the future, the New Jersey based attorney told her not to do it on the East Coast, but in California where the paperwork would be handled for less than $50.

By this time, Steve was in a bit of a panic because he knew that for quite some time Ida had been fed up with him for not working hard enough and she needed change. She had been feeling that it would be easier to be single and that was not good news for their marriage. She needed a partner, not a man who didn't carry his weight.

When Ida gave notice at Johnson & Johnson, it was a big deal as the company didn't appreciate her resignation. The company was one of those entities where you worked for a lifetime, and you didn't just quit unless you retired or died. Well, she was neither retired nor dead. Instead she wanted to build a successful career and was still figuring out how. The news of Ida's departure spread like wildfire. Within hours, thousands of people who worked there knew about it. Workers were shocked that a refugee had the guts to leave the place. Some even mocked and put Ida down, implying that she didn't appreciate the corporation enough. Some suggested she was going to Hollywood to be the next Zsazsa Gabor. The truth was that Ida had a similar accent, but she never had the inkling to be an actress or be in front of the camera. Even though she admired the profession and performers' unbelievable ability to transform, Ida's heart was somewhere else.

Ida waited for the kids' school year to end and then she packed up the whole family and began the journey to California. Even though Steve didn't originally want to move anywhere, he was now more than ready to join them. The only thing Ida intended to take with them was her dog and cat, but she ended up shipping them to Irene's address instead. While the pets flew to the West Coast, the Csiszars took a cross-country trip.

CHAPTER SEVEN

The City of Warm Golden Peach

(USA – West Coast: 1973–Today)

7. USA – West Coast: Summer of 1973 – Today

Irene had been living in the City of Angels for a while and liked the area very much. She was the one who originally came up with the notion that Ida should relocate to L.A. Irene was working for the famous department store, Bullock's, in Beverly Hills. She told Ida that if she moved out to the West Coast, she'd hire her as a buyer so she would have a job upon arrival.

When they got to the Golden State on a sunny summer day it was pleasantly warm, the sky was blue, and the dark cloud of separation had dissipated. Ida and Steve stayed with Irene and John while looking for a house.

Unfortunately, it became apparent that Bullock's where Irene was working was closing its doors and possibly relocating to the San Fernando Valley, a suburb of the megapolis, so Ida decided to look elsewhere.

One crucial item on Ida's to-do list was to find a new physician for her circulatory and blood issues; one who could adjust the latest dose of her medication. Irene's M.D., once again, saved the day. Ida's visit fell on a Tuesday morning so, as usual, she dressed up like a world-class dame and headed to the medical office. After a blood test, he determined that her condition was back to normal, and she could stop taking her prescription altogether. While waiting for her results, the physician casually inquired what Ida did on the East Coast. She shared that she worked in the quality control department for Johnson & Johnson's for a decade and she was looking for a position in the area. The practitioner was so impressed with her background that he immediately picked up the phone and said into the receiver: "Hey Paul, I found you a technician! You need to see her right away; this is a doctor's order." Whoever Paul was, Ida was curious to meet him.

Mr. Paul Benes was the doctor's best friend, patient, and most importantly, he was the famous Hollywood movie make-up, Max Factor & Company's key personnel. The actual numbers might help to understand how big the international corporation was: in 1973, the company sold for US$500 million (approximately $2.9 billion in 2017 dollars). Mr. Benes was the very person who trained employees to develop quality makeup. He had been looking for and complaining about not being able to find the person who had the right mixture of knowledge, dedication, and skill to live up to the demanding position—one whom he could train correctly. He had been complaining long enough that his friend remembered this when he met Ida.

The practitioner gave her Mr. Benes' address and Ida was on her way to an interview. By the time she got there, five staff members were already waiting for her. The position had been vacant for so long, they were more eager than Ida was. Her superb beige suit, shiny high heels, and cherry lipstick revealed that she certainly had a balanced sense of aesthetics. As the slim-figured woman with platinum hair walked towards the reception area, she definitely made an impression that was in alignment with the image of the star-focused beauty industry.

After her initial meeting, the representative gave Ida her phone number and mentioned that she'd be calling her at some point. Arriving home, Ida barely walked through the door when the phone rang. "Mrs. Csiszar, can you start tomorrow morning?"

She was incredibly excited to have immediately landed a position. After hanging up the receiver, she could hardly wait to share the big news with her family, but she got interrupted. The human resources department was calling again. "Mrs. Csiszar, we forgot to discuss your salary..." Ida was offered $10,000 more than she was making at Johnson & Johnson! And, she wasn't making bad money there either! When her previous coworkers heard that she had immediately landed a job with Max Factor, they couldn't believe the Tinsel Town story. Ida was definitely moving forward and upward in life and she felt exuberant! She perceived that she was increasingly blessed by a higher power; God seemed to have held her hand and guided her in the right direction.

Her employment started with a tour of all the facilities during which she met several welcoming and warm Hungarian staff members. Historically, Hungarians have a strong work ethic; having another country(wo)man on the team was good news for everyone. Though no matter how good they were, they had probably not seen the extraordinary speed and outstanding problem-solving skills Ida brought with her.

Working at Max Factor was like being in a candy store. Mr. Benes became Ida's professional hero; he was her miracle man. She liked and respected him tremendously, although in the beginning it took her a while to get used to his pushy, hands-on management style.

FULFILLING MY AMERCIAN DREAM!

He was always close by as their desks were not far apart. The big one was his, the small one was hers.

He had good reason to be continuously crowding her: he saw a unique talent in Ida and, like a good coach, he kept applying pressure on her to learn more, understand more, expand more. At times, it was overwhelming when he explained things repeatedly, but in a beauty industry lab, it was crucial that our budding liquid chemist understood how the various materials, chemical structures, silicon endings on the molecules interacted with each other and why. She also needed to see which ingredients were used for which products and what their exact functions were. It was a tremendous amount of information that Ida needed to acquire before assisting with the creation of lipsticks, mascaras, eye shadows, and foundations.

Everything went relatively well until one day Ida's mixture burst into large flames. "See, I told you that you need to know what you're doing!" Mr. Benes said. After wiping her tears away, she got right back to it, because in the end, all she wanted was being able to create on her own. Ida was grateful that he made her experiment a lot; in the long run it served her well. Practicing chemistry, using her sense of beauty, and inventing on her own was Ida's ultimate goal. It seemed that she found the right position in the right industry to realize her dreams.

At one point, Ida thought she really knew everything, but then he took her education to another level. He made her cool, heat, and freeze all the samples to demonstrate that they behaved differently at various temperatures. Ida needed to observe all the displayed characteristics of each component, as well as their reaction time— an important factor for creating cosmetics.

Makeup chemistry was considered "try chemistry" which meant that she needed to experience not just the individual elements but also how they functioned together in a cohesive manner once it was put on the skin. The only way to do that was by trying.

Beauty products are subjective, and at the time, they were made exclusively for women.

When Ida created a new concoction, she had to put herself in the shoes of her customers and use her ability to feel empathetically, so she would anticipate how *they* would perceive the product. She had to go beyond science, be open and in a receptive mood, so her personal experience of the new mix would be infused into it. Depending on the goal, Ida also had to figure out several other aspects such as the gloss factor. There were so many different types of waxes she could use, but to make a quality stick with the appropriate shininess—that would both feel luscious on one's lips and glide efficiently—was trial and error by applying various substances. The colors and textures could also change day to day. One day it could feel slippery and the next day dry. The mixture could change overnight so the laboratory technicians needed to keep the formulas and recipes neat and organized otherwise they couldn't reproduce the same exact chemical structures. The methodology of shipping was another element as was the weather. A cargo to sunny Arizona was a different ball game than sending makeup to cold Canada. Ida had to pay close attention to the metallic aspects as well, especially when creating eye shadows. To avoid being greasy when one blinks, the speed of drying time had to be short as you cannot expect a customer to keep their eyes closed just to wait for the powder to dry. In the case of beauty products, balancing aesthetics with functionality was crucial: makeup served the needs and comfort of the users and not the other way around.

Slowly, but surely, Ida learned what the components' functionalities were. Mr. Benes kept repeating and repeating the information, and then making her repeat what he said back to him. After a while Ida had enough and said: "Mr. Benes, I know already!" "Nah! Trust me, you know nothing!" In hindsight, she indeed hardly knew anything about the profession.

After a year, she was starting to doubt that she'd ever acquire all the insights to succeed in the industry when Mr. Benes announced that he was going on a long vacation and would see her in three

months. "But Mr. Benes!" Ida said, "I don't know what to do!?"
"Yes, you do! You now know very well what do to!" he
responded. Ready or not, Ida was suddenly on her own. "By the
way," he said on his way out, "While I'm gone, the big desk will
be your new place."

So, Mr. Benes took off for his European holiday, and indeed Ida
knew what to do. Before he left, he took her on a couple of
industrial tours inside the factory and gave her a key to the
company car so that temporarily she could do Mr. Benes' job and
supervise the next phase of the product's life while he was gone.

In the laboratory, Ida always mixed small samples but now she was
asked to be part of the factory's subsequent step: increasing and
testing a 100 lbs. pilot batch thoroughly before they started to mix
an even larger size of 1000 lbs. of liquid. While one would think
that chemicals in small quantities behave the same way as big
quantities; in the case of makeup it's not so, and percentages need
to be adjusted.

Before the team started experimenting with larger volumes, they needed the marketing department's stamp of approval. The particular product for which five new shades were being developed needed to be supervised by Ida. This meant that she had to drive to the manufacturing facility located in an area which was not particularly safe. The first time she went there alone, she was trembling with fear. However, she got herself together quickly, concealing her fright, and she walked in there with the confidence of a general.

The factory was operated with union workers which meant Ida was not allowed to touch anything, which for her energetic personality was very foreign. On the other hand, she was allowed to give instruction to the workers on what they were to do. Initially, they didn't have much respect for her because everyone knew she was a rookie, so they tested her to see how far they could go with their defiance. Ida requested that all five shades be blended that day, but the workers were slow, took all sorts of breaks, and made her wait.

She got annoyed, so during their lunch break, she married all of the ingredients for all of the shades by herself. Coming back from their meal, it was now the laborers who were upset. They told her that, per union rules, she may not do again what she just did. "Tell it to the union!" she responded. "And, do not ever challenge me again!" she added. She then grabbed the samples and delivered them to the home office by 2 PM. The next morning the marketing department approved every one of them and the colors went into production. Of course, no union representative ever contacted Ida about the incident, and from then on, each time she went to the compounding warehouse, she was called names behind her back. Ida didn't care though, because if she ever did, she would have never gotten anywhere in life.

Eventually she did make a dear friend at the factory, Frank Vadasz Uncle Frank, as she called him with much affection, always helped her out when she needed to alter a shade. While others were having lunch, he snuck in the right ingredients to correct the color. Today, so many years later, Ida still exchanges Christmas cards with this man who has surpassed the ripe old age of one hundred. Ida sends holiday cards to all of her former boss; she is loyal that way.

Even though she wasn't popular with everyone, it didn't take years before Ida became a well-liked person at Max Factor's central office. She was offered a promotion, but—to everyone's surprise—she refused! Being the fair person, she had always been, she knew that she was the youngest and others had for long been in line for a higher position. She didn't feel it would be just for her to cut in front of everyone else even though the management thought she earned it.

Ida worked at the speed of light, at least compared to the other four workers with whom she shared the laboratory, and because of this, she was especially appreciated by the marketing department. If Ida was involved, they didn't need to wait to get their next item off their agenda. She never made anyone stand by for weeks to finish a project or days to mix a color. Rather, she would develop a hue within four to five hours. Because of her efficiency, she always had a stack of tasks on her desk while others had two to three, at the most.

One day, a marketing director invited Ida to lunch at her Beverly Hills house; she was interested in working more closely with Ida. Her residence had a beautiful garden and the pigmentations of the roses were unique, so the executive proposed for Ida to recreate them. They cut off six blossoms for Ida to take back as samples and by the next morning, she was ready to present all the freshly mixed samples!

Unlike others, Ida hardly ever procrastinated. What really made her shine though was her exceptional talent for copying shades and creating inviting luscious makeup products. It seems easy to see a color and construct it from scratch, but in reality, it's as challenging as writing down a symphony after hearing it only once. A hue can have so many undertones; seeing them for what they are and analyzing its components cannot be learned. You are either born with that talent or you aren't.

FULFILLING MY
AMERCIAN DREAM!

In today's beauty industry, there are precise formulas that technicians can follow, so there is hardly any need for a visual talent like Ida's. All the same, back in the days when chemicals and color blueprints for each beauty product mixed from raw materials and from scratch, Ida's exceptional talent was immeasurable and greatly admired.

At Max Factor, there was a hierarchical approval system in place. Nearly everything had to be rubber-stamped and most of the time getting permission seemed to take forever. Once, Ida spotted a gigantic pile waiting to be green lit on her boss' desk, she was apprehensive about her concepts ever going anywhere, because her boss' signature was needed, confirming that he completed the mandatory review and said "yes" to her idea. Since Ida wasn't exactly a woman who was willing to take no for an answer, she had to get inventive about how to get around her manager. "Better to ask for forgiveness than permission" -- with this motto, she introduced the notion that she would fake his signature, with his knowledge, so that she then could submit her designs to the next level. Ida thought it was an excellent idea! After all, it saved time for him and her. Upon reproducing his autograph, she showed it to him, making sure he thought it looked similar enough, and then they laughed about it!

Now she was ready to submit her plan to the person above him—figuratively and literally speaking. The supervisor was also the president of the department who oversaw the ninth, tenth, and eleventh floor in—what they called—the Tower. This building was across from the famous Chinese Theater on Hollywood Boulevard with all the cemented hand and footprints of movie stars. Ida asked for and got an appointment to present her project. This was a daring move that brought her a tremendous amount of success as time went on.

Eventually, her reputation became such that if the company wanted to get something completed or corrected quickly, they asked Ida to jump on it. As a matter of fact, as the corporation started to really trust her, she no longer needed any approval from anyone. This was perfect for her, because she'd never liked being controlled or told what to do. Both, Max Factor and Ida, benefited from granting her the professional freedom to do her own thing.

During her time there, she sat in on plenty of meetings, created many formulas, and above all, got all jobs done well. By far, she was the most expeditious employee and accordingly, Ida was given the nickname "Super Chicken." While she was good with all beauty products, her favorites were lipsticks and lip glosses in which she excelled.

Ida began to feel deeply respected by and cherished at the company due to her hard work, dedication, and swiftness. At her review with the big boss, she was told that she was "Max Factor's pillar" and he suggested yet another raise. After five years she had the impression that her salary was significantly higher than other employees' who had worked there much longer. Frequently, she received additional weighty bonuses. For Christmas, it was not unusual for her to receive a $1,000 bonus which in 2017 was worth $6,300. When she opened her holiday envelope and she noticed an extra check attached to her regular check; it was indeed a Merry Christmas!

During her employment there, buyers would let Ida know about new raw materials that had become available on the market. They would also educate her about how they were applied and for what they were used. Ida would frequently experiment with and incorporate these fresh components into her new formulas and would come up with modern products not yet seen by any other beauty product producers. For her to develop these new mixtures, she had to simultaneously wear two hats: one of the chemist's and one of the marketers. Inventing unfamiliar blends was one of the most lucrative things Ida did for Max Factor, even though she didn't seriously benefit financially from the fruits of her labor. Nevertheless, she enjoyed the development process so much that she regularly stayed after 5 PM which was the end of the work day

FULFILLING MY AMERCIAN DREAM!

Once 7 PM passed, security would frequently pester Ida to go home so they could finally lock up the building and have dinner.

No matter how great a place Max Factor was, there were always some people who wanted to work elsewhere. When Ida learned that a person was leaving for another manufacturer, she would give them her phone number, so they maintained their connections. By keeping in touch with former coworkers and utilizing her outstanding interpersonal skills, Ida eventually developed her own personal network. This not only contributed to her success but resulted in additional important connections. She got to know the make-up artist for Tom Cruise and Nicole Kidman, and other major Hollywood stars. Ida was even invited to go to the Oscars by Rachel Perry, an actress who had her own makeup line and became Ida's client. But Ida has never been interested in the spotlight, so she decided not to attend. By that time, she heard that her former employer, Johnson & Johnson, had finally acknowledged her achievements! Ida was recognized as the master chemist at Max Factor and was a star in her industry!

FULFILLING MY AMERCIAN DREAM!

When Max Factor decided to leave California behind for the East Coast, many employees moved with the company, but not Ida. She wanted to stay on the West Coast, so they offered her a severance package of $50,000. She felt her 15 years with the big brand name was her real university and it proved to be one of the most memorable times of her life.

Ida had always dreamed of having her own business, but she was not clear as to whether she wanted to have her own makeup line, or if she was going to produce cosmetics for other major brands. But one thing she knew for sure: she wanted to own a factory one way or the other.

While at Max Factor, she found out that the Hollywood corporation occasionally had too much work or too big of an order so they farmed out the workload to a certain New Jersey company. This sub-contractor also assisted other well-known beauty lines to produce their cosmetics for them. As far as Ida knew, this manufacturer was the only one that could fulfill such requests for other corporations. Apparently, they had international divisions as well and they could produce cosmetics for anyone and anywhere around the world. This is how the idea of developing and producing cosmetics for already established companies popped into Ida's head. This was an easier path toward profit than having her own makeup line, so this notion stayed with her for years to come. Once she left Max Factor, it seemed like a perfect time to roll up her sleeves and make it happen.

Ida's first attempt was ViDa which she launched with a previous coworker. For 18 months they tried working together, but the coworker didn't live up to Ida's expectations. Her partner didn't have any business sense, and it was left to Ida to do most of the work. Their enterprise was far from fun, fair, or lucrative. In 18 months, they had hardly made any progress, so Ida decided to cut her losses and move on. Except that by this time, the woman owed Ida $150,000 and she didn't have the money to pay it back. Ida suggested that her associate continue working for her as a form of payment and do so based on Ida's recipes, mixing mascaras, lipsticks, and eye shadows in bulk.

At the time, Irene owned a printing company and there was a 1,000 square foot attic they allowed Ida to use for her second venture. When Ida's network heard that her colleague had finally left the business, they sought her out and were ready to contract her new entity, La Prestige.

Regardless of her drive and interest, this time, Ida wasn't as confident as she was when she kicked off ViDa. She felt discouraged and was no longer convinced that she was doing the right thing. She went so far as toying with the idea of getting a regular job again. On the other hand, she kept reminding herself as to why she wanted to have her own business: deep down she felt she was equipped for it, in spite of the fact that throughout the years there were plenty of people who doubted her. Was her thought process just wishful thinking or would she really be able to build an enterprise? She was wondering what direction to take, after all, she was just a small-town foreigner whose English wasn't perfect, and she still felt she wasn't American enough. She vacillated about it for weeks. Was she too old to pursue her dream? Perhaps she was; she was already approaching fifty... Regardless of all the obstacles she was facing, she still wanted to prove herself to herself, as well as to the world. Because she kept receiving so much encouragement from her broadening network, close friends, and immediate family, she decided to leave her doubts behind and just go for it.

Since she no longer had a partner, she was doing all the work herself and still able to deliver about $20,000 worth of products monthly. She started to feel more positive and her growing compensation was promising. Ida was not yet where she imagined herself to be but then an angel with an unexpected offer appeared...

Lajos, yet another doctor of Irene's who also took are of Ida and Steve, proposed to be Ida's business partner. He said he had been observing her business conduct for a while, admiring her high level of professionalism, and outstanding interpersonal skills, he offered to be her angel investor. He had a few years before his retirement and genuinely wanted to help Ida succeed. He saw an opportunity for both him and her. The proposition caught Ida off guard and when he asked her how much money she needed, she was struggling to find the right answer. Her severance package was partially gone because Steve was on disability again. She already refinanced their house, which they did regularly, while trying to build a business. It was a risky and temporary solution but their only certain financial resource. She finally blurted out a number: $50,000. After some thinking she realized she needed $500,000 instead but it was too late to renegotiate. Just the equipment she needed cost millions of dollars, but Ida wasn't going to be stopped by such minor details as having no appliances.

She told Lajos she wanted to start simply, but in a bigger place, so they rented a bigger, 2,000 square foot space. He didn't know anything about makeup or what they needed, but Ida educated him so they could have informed discussions about what was necessary for their growth. Ida found outlets and auctions where she could get her hands-on used machines that were still in good condition as well as raw materials, tools, boxes, and so-called baking essentials. With Steve's help, she visited industrial depots and purchased large containers, grinders, and mixers. The men installed the equipment for her on the new property and she got to work.

In some of the buckets she bought used, she found random beauty products. She identified the manufacturers and contacted them for additional information, so that she could learn, grow, and proposition them to order from her. She gained customers by being an extraordinary negotiator with old world charm and having a distinctive and recognizable accent which set her apart from others. Within five years the enterprise was blooming. Getting an account by Jafra Cosmetics International, was a major milestone. Their headquarters were in Westlake Village, California, close to Ida's office. After delivering an order of 1,200 lbs. of lipstick, her client transported the liquid to their new manufacturing facility in

Queretaro, a north-central state in Mexico, to pour it in its final shape, and then box it up for sale.

While labor was cheaper south of the border, finding an expert to manage the process from alpha to omega was a problem. They asked whether Ida would fly to Mexico and assist with establishing the finishing process. Her daily compensation was $1000 in addition to first class travel. Once she completed that task, Jafra realized they had to get more equipment, specific to the needs of that particular facility, and again there was no one who had the expertise to supervise the expensive purchases. Ida's presence was requested the second time around. For two and a half years, she commuted back and forth between Los Angeles and Mexico City, while simultaneously running her own company in California. She usually spent a week in Queretaro and then a week in the U.S. but after a while she started to feel exhausted from overextending herself for such a prolonged period of time.

If that was not enough responsibility, Ida also started working with

a former Max Factor employee who had opened his own luxury

cosmetic shop in Beverly Hills manufacturing custom-made

lipsticks. Clients could bring in any item of any color, and Ida

would recreate the object's hue for their makeup order. It was not

unusual to match underwear, swimming suits, and rather strange

things… The orders were pouring in to the point that Ida could not

keep up. She wanted to find a way to leverage her system, so she

created a color chart that listed each ingredient and quantity so that

the technicians could mix the hue. Once she put it together in a

written guide, she trained the workers how to mix the raw

materials, oils, and waxes. It took a long time for them to acquire

the process because it takes much more than just numbers and

charts. As a chemist, one needs to know how to efficiently

substitute a shade when the exact color is not available or utilize

another raw material if the lab runs ran out of the original

ingredient.

FULFILLING MY AMERCIAN DREAM!

By creating a blueprint for Visage, she basically gave away her invention away for pennies. This very act reveals how much Ida was ahead of her time: today, decades later, the beauty companies manufacture based on exact and detailed formulas. Back then, due to Ida's leveraging, Visage grew exponentially and became an extremely successful enterprise, expanding from one location to many stores nationwide. Sadly, when its owner was struck with AIDS, his health started to deteriorate rapidly. Before his passing he sold his company; it was rumored that he received $110 million dollars from Revlon.

When the brand's new owner learned about Ida's charts, her name and reputation skyrocketed in a New York minute not just with them, but across the beauty industry. Revlon invited Ida to work for them but no matter how good that sounded, she was committed to running her own factory. Well, if they couldn't have her on premises, they still wanted her off premises. Ida got a two-year lipstick contract with them to work on the shades that Revlon bought from Visage.

FULFILLING MY
AMERCIAN DREAM!

Originally, when Ida went independent, she had no machines, so she manually mixed all of her 10-20-pound orders in ordinary cooking pots on a regular stove. Now, she was taking on 2,000 to 3,000-pound lipstick contracts which presented its challenges. While the big accounts were wonderful news, suddenly, she needed to upgrade her facility. She needed to purchase larger mixing containers and expand the space. She also decided to change the name of her company: La Prestige was out, Classic Cosmetics was in.

After seven years of having the pleasure of Lajos' financial and business support, he was ready to depart as an investor. He received two million dollars from Ida which she was more than happy to pay the man who saw and believed the great potential in her like no one else did.

When Max Factor moved to the East Coast, there were a couple of employees who went to work for the Estee Lauder brand that was also named after an American business woman who was of Hungarian origin. Ida contacted her previous coworkers when she found what a well-known company they were working for, and that's how Classic Cosmetics ended up securing a contract with one of the biggest companies in the beauty industry.

Because Ida and Estee Lauder shared their Eastern European roots, Ida has always had some curiosity about the industry mogul. While she never had the chance to meet her personally, she did meet one of her sons later in life. It happened that Classic Cosmetics had a working relationship with a company, named Stilla, which was bought up by the Estee Lauder Companies, who then became Ida's client again. In connection with the account, Ms. Lauder's son came to visit Los Angeles and Ida had a chance to have a delightful conversation with him.

There were other star brands that eventually came trough Ida's door such as L'Oréal and Victoria Jackson Makeup. The latter had been a memorable name in the makeup industry as for 30 years it was one of QVC's favorite brands.

As Classic Cosmetics grew, Ida finally started to see the fruits of her labor. Truthfully, no successful business person's history is without setbacks and that's true for Ida as well. When Ida received the devastating message, she dropped everything: her younger son, Frank, had lymphoma and he wasn't even yet 30! There was a growing lump on his head and Frank needed both treatments: chemotherapy and radiation. Ida was hit by the news incredibly hard. For the first time in a long time she picked up the Bible and prayed like she had never prayed before, because she hurt like she had never hurt before.

She begged God not to take her son away. Every. Single. Day. Meanwhile, Frank decided to live his life, whatever was left of it, to its fullest. Ida knew that Frank had always wanted to have a Harley, so after the diagnosis was revealed, she went to the store and bought him one. The first time Frankie, as his mother called him, rode his new motorcycle was to his first chemotherapy appointment. He was going to enjoy every minute of his days to come. He travelled, went skiing, and didn't let cancer slow down his accelerated tempo. At most, he took an hour to rest after a treatment, but then went back to work and continued marching through the weeks and months to come until he started to get better.

In the midst of this, Ida was searching for answers and building a relationship with God. She started to believe more profoundly than before, and for the first time since she left the atheist Communist propaganda behind, was reading the Bible every morning. She put her spiritual thoughts on paper in her little bordeaux-colored notebook and her daily discussions with the higher power were becoming a habit. She would randomly open her scripture and study different parts, and this became a form of mediation. She found her quiet, 6 AM ritual uplifting, inspiring, and calming. The most important part of her practice was to thank the Almighty every day for being a blessed person, because after Frank's cancer was in remission that's exactly what she felt she was a blessed person. She also renewed her friendships with those who had similar beliefs so they could exchange thoughts and notes with each other. Ida carefully kept her writings because she hoped that one day her children would give them to someone who could benefit from them.

Regardless of her Christian book-learning, which she has been practicing ever since, she never really felt particularly religious. She did feel a very strong connection to God, although she only went to church on holidays, unless she was visiting Hungary, where she attended services multiple times a week. She loved the hymns from her childhood, accordingly she revisited those intermittently not just when she was by herself but when she was around her extended family back in Gyoma.

During one of her early visits to her motherland, she spotted a book of psalms in the church. It was used, it was old, but it was dear. Other devotees wrote various sweet comments in it and from then on, every time she attended a service, she too added some notes of devotion. Year after year, she was able to find the popular copy where she had previously left it. It grew close to her heart and eventually, she asked the pastor whether he would permit her to bring it back to the U.S. She kept making notes in it and when she ran out of space, she requested a professional book binder to add more blank pages to the back and she continued jotting down her theological thoughts. She also asked her sister, Irene, to enrich the book which continues to mean a lot to Ida especially because it's from her birth town, Gyoma.

Since she had been gone from Hungary an entire generation had grown up without being exposed to the concept of a higher power. Ida felt that they were missing out and that frowning upon the idea of God shortchanged many. She had felt the a Almighty's guidance all of her life and she was grateful that she was able to get closer to Him. During her visits to her homeland, she convinced her family members to get baptized even if they were already adults. Carrying on the Gal's tradition, eventually all of her siblings' children got christened and went through the confirmation process as well. Ida continued to encourage her loved ones to keep their faith strong and alive, and she prayed for them at night before she turned off the lights.

While Ida was going through her own emotional crisis during her son's sickness, Steve also struggled with it even if he didn't show it. Seeing what cancer treatment does to a body, after four decades of smoking, he decided to quit the destructive habit for good. Having gone through such a traumatic experience together, Ida and Steve both grew stronger individually as well as a couple.

They continued working together at Classic Cosmetics, a family-owned and family-oriented, employee and immigrant-friendly operation. They were very involved in their enterprise that they built from the ground up. Within the company, they both found their roles rewarding and that made them feel needed, fulfilled and proud. Steve was not a good businessman, consequently he let Ida be the leader, after all it was her brainchild to begin with. That didn't mean that he was a weak man—he would put down his foot when he had to—but he did have a different strong suit. Steve was the engineer of the company who conscientiously fixed and maintained the machinery which kept their workplace running smoothly and efficiently. He didn't have an actual degree, but he had a fantastic affinity for finding creative solutions for mechanical problems. He was not afraid to get his hands dirty if necessary. He too worked hard and went to the factory almost every weekend to make sure that everything was satisfactory on the premises.

Steve was also the cheerful soul of Classic Cosmetics as he focused on interpersonal relationships. He was congenial with their employees—he knew everyone's name, and personally greeted each individual in each department every single morning. He tried to put a smile on their faces and made an effort to inquire about the workers' children and their problems. The personnel appreciated that tremendously. People don't remember him ever raising his voice. Instead, he was a fun, charming, easy-to-approach gentleman that everybody sincerely loved.

Ida, on the other hand, was hard on people, at least from an American point of view. Her matter of fact, no-filter, Eastern European verbal communication, didn't translate well. She wasn't trying to be harsh or offensive, just wanted to get to the point; she wanted to demonstrate how well things could be done. Ida wanted all of the products to be perfect as they came out the door, because she was looking to create a recognized company. In order to do that, she needed to watch her dollars, and ensure that the lines were running expeditiously, but not so quickly that the products would get damaged. She would speed up the assembly line and tell the employees to work faster. This was considered the most unusual aspect about Ida's management style. She was often frustrated as her own innate work ethic was really hard to come by in others. She wasn't a screamer, but she commanded the room. Her way of running the business drove all people to respect her, some to fear her, many to like her, and plenty to adore her.

Ida was an "alpha female" before the term was widely used. She was the driving force of Classic Cosmetics and her passion was contagious. She was tenacious and once she set her mind on her goal, she was going to get there no matter what. There wasn't a job she was unwilling to do. At the onset, she had to juggle many plates because she couldn't afford to have a full staff. Simultaneously, she had to be the chief executive officer, customer service representative, compounder, and sales specialist in which, of course, she excelled. If a customer came in and wanted to order something Ida didn't know how to do, she would not stop until she figured it out. While staying the course she never had to compromise her integrity; she has never been the person who stepped on others to move forward. Her strength, logical thinking, independent nature, and saying what was what, made her the boss.

Ida and Steve put in a tremendous amount of time and effort into building their successful enterprise. While Ida was the face of the corporation, Steve was right behind her. They worked really well together, and they were a powerful team. They were also committed advocates of work-life balance and together they created a work environment with substantial benefits that included health; dental; life; Aflac insurance; notable vacation time; free appreciation lunches; pizza parties; Thanksgiving turkeys; Good Fridays off, and lots of flexibility regarding personal leave. Taking time off for sick children, doctor appointments, graduations was acceptable to management if the privilege was not abused. As long as people put in their eight hours, the company allowed late arrivals and early departures as many of the parents had to design their schedules around their kids' school. The company also made sure that they didn't interrupt their staff's off hours at night or on holidays as there is no such thing as a "lipstick emergency".

Having a kid-friendly work environment was something of which Ida was particularly proud. As she was growing into the role of an accomplished entrepreneur, she was becoming seriously "cool" as a couple of kindergarteners described her. When her main chemist brought her daughters in, Ida promptly led them into the lab. After seating the girls in the high chairs, dressing them up in lab coats, giving them colors along with some food flavoring to create their own makeup, the kiddos had an incredible amount of fun and from then on thought that their mom had the best job in the whole wide world.

Remembering how Ida and Steve had to work around family and health issues themselves, they wanted to demonstrate true care for their employees' and their loved ones' well-being. No wonder Classic Cosmetics has many long-time employees who have been there for decades. The retention rate that peaked at 70% was something Ida consciously worked for, as she knew her company was only as good as her employees. As one would expect, the gradual but consistent increase in production reflected her win-win philosophy which served Classic Cosmetics well.

There have been many occasions when Ida was extraordinarily generous with her employees. When she hired people from Gyoma and sponsored their green cards, she provided them with a lifetime opportunity. Also, if asked, she gave jobs to the children of her friends. When a staff member went to Mexico and was hospitalized for a month due to a near drowning accident, the company kept her position open for her and assisted her with getting back to the U.S. When a worker's child got seriously ill, the employees put together an emergency fund that Classic Cosmetics matched.

Ida's care extended not just to individuals, but to smaller companies that she helped grow, and it paid off! Her name became known worldwide, although that was never the reason for her generosity. When she started her business, it she was one of the first factories of this type on the West Coast and being the first one in anything is a big deal. Her current success is based on how many years she has been in the business.

At Classic Cosmetics, the corporation's motto is posted on the walls: "Quality is the responsibility of every employee. Customer satisfaction is our goal." The compounders do a phenomenal job, their products are superb.

FULFILLING MY AMERCIAN DREAM!

Besides quality, speed is their other focus. In the beauty industry, it is crucial to deliver on time because the products are usually tied to a nationwide or even international marketing campaigns with a preset and specific public launch date. If the manufacturer is behind, it could cost the brand millions of dollars and most importantly cause many disappointed customers. Their big-name clients expect perfection and Classic Cosmetics honestly does their very best to live up to it. The corporation is known for delivering in a timely fashion and for that punctuality their purchasers are willing to pay the price. They have never been the least expensive on the market, but with them you get the level of professionalism that you expect and pay for it.

Ida has never allowed any animal testing in her factory, and as the public's demand grew, Classic Cosmetics started to produce some organic, semi-organic, and environmentally-friendly lines. These green products had their own challenges though the less synthetic an ingredient was, the less its functionality could be controlled.

That was not good news for a company who guaranteed consistency. While it was true that ingredients could be switched out, frequently the product's performance—especially when high and intense colors were fashionable—could be compromised.

As Ida's company was expanding, so did her family. Both of her married sons started to have children of their own. Back when Ida launched Classic Cosmetics, her first grandchild was born, and Ida was ecstatic to have a grandson, Danny! Little did she know that she'd soon have four more. Soon after, Cory was born, then Devin, after that Austin, and then her youngest grandson, Shane.

Around the same time, as the natural cycle of life goes, Ida lost her parents. They both passed away in their 80s after having lived long and eventful lives. They left this earth knowing that their daughter, Ida, had made something of herself.

Ida's children, Steven and Frank were also advancing professionally. Steve, a talkative and well-read extrovert, got his

Bachelor of Science in engineering, and his master's degree in finance. He secured a job with NASA and worked on missile launches as a top-secret space engineer.

Frank, a tall and warm-hearted introvert with a great sense of humor, had a background in welding and originally was an aircraft mechanic and machinist. Then he had a change of heart and started working for Classic Cosmetics and found that he absolutely loved being around his parents; it made his days so much better. He was learning the nuances of the beauty industry and slowly advanced within the company.

In his mid 30s, Steven too got into the beauty industry. His parents asked their older son to join the company and while he was thrilled, he also felt that he would rather do it on his own. With the seed money he received from his mother and father, he established West Coast Cosmetics, and just like his mother, bought his own factory. Ida gave Steven her biggest account and that client alone brought him $6 millions dollars annually. Ida also had certain clients who already had their own packaging, and what they needed was to fill them up with whatever color or material they had left over from previous orders or auctions. Classic Cosmetics molded the raw material they purchased in mass quantities from various outlets and sold them to these particular customers who then sold the makeup to Europe, China, and other countries around the world. Just these accounts by themselves were so much work they could hardly fulfill the orders. Once Ida saw that Steven was handling business well, she was happy to pass these accounts over to West Coast Cosmetics and he was happy to take them. His clients were satisfied, and his work ethic was identical to Ida's, so she was more than confident to pass on additional clients to Steven.

Classic Cosmetics and West Coast Cosmetics were similar in nature; the only difference was their size and the clientele they served. Steven liked his business because he produced tangible products and Frank liked becoming a pillar of the company because he was surrounded by wonderful people. Ida felt pleased that she was able to provide both of her sons with a solid financial foundation to get a decent start in life—that has been greatly appreciated by both Steven and Frank.

Keeping the family's philosophy to "be the best person you can be" alive, the two sons have always been there for each other: whether it was needing some raw material, fixing a broken part, or borrowing an employee. Leading a nice life while being a decent human being was something they carried on in their personal as well as professional lives.

Once Steven's company was gaining a solid reputation in the field of beauty, people started to confuse him with his father, as originally, he was going by "Steve" as well. To make matters more complicated, both companies were located in Chatsworth, CA. They even went to the same pharmacy, so plenty of times Steven would get a call to pick up his medication, just to get there to realize it was not his but his father's! So, mix-ups were plenty!

FULFILLING MY AMERCIAN DREAM!

Steven knew things had to change, and one particular emergency made the need immediate.

One day the local hospital phoned Steven that his father had been rushed to the cardiology department with a heart problem and he should come right away. Speeding as fast as he could, upon his arrival he announced himself: "I'm Steve, I'm here!" "Hurry!" the nurse said, handing him a gown. "Get undressed!" she added. He started to disrobe quickly down to his birthday suit thinking his father was dying and the frail man wanted to leave him with some last words of wisdom. "But why did they want *me* in a Johnny?" he suddenly wondered and then asked. "Because you will be operated on!" the physician's assistant responded. Indeed, Mr. Csiszar needed to get an urgent procedure done, but not Steven but Steve, Ida's husband! That's when Steven realized it was time to change his name.

Given that Ida's marriage ended up lasting for 55 years—in which she was the heart and Steve was the soul—it was intensely painful for Ida to witness both of her sons go through divorce. Since neither of her former daughter-in-laws were Hungarian, none of the grandchildren were taught much about their heritage. Ida decided to take an active part in assisting her sons, who were raised to continue their linguistic, cultural, and culinary customs as well as identify as Hungarian-Americans, to help inspire their children to carry on their heritage and language which Steven and Frank both spoke. Ida bought a smaller mansion in Gyoma so that any of the grandchildren could regularly go home any time. She herself took three of them to visit Hungary and wants to take the rest of them when they are ready. Her cultural missionary work seemed to have worked because later on when Ida had her first and only great granddaughter (up to the time of this writing), even though the young child hadn't even started elementary school, she already identified as Hungarian. Ida frequently talked to her in Hungarian and brought her a folk dress, with lots of pretty and colorful flowers, that the little girl loved. When she grew out of it, she was as upset as a seriously upset four-year old can be!

FULFILLING MY AMERCIAN DREAM!

Besides assuring that her grand and great grandchildren had a place to stay in her motherland, she also had, as always, several business ideas for her mansion. Because the manor was close to rivers, forests, and spas, Ida thought it was going to make an international year-around tourist center and an excellent getaway for nature lovers. Hungary's distinctively different four seasons offered endless possibilities for visitors. She was hoping to recreate the area's turn of the 20th century charm and expand upon it by purchasing another old and romantic castle nearby, and then renovate it according to current Western standards.

She wanted to involve her sister and relatives residing in Hungary and make it a Gal enterprise but, unfortunately, none of her family members wanted to jump on the opportunity to develop her concept. By including them she was hoping to spread the wealth while she stayed with her master creation, Classic Cosmetics, which in a way was everything to her.

FULFILLING MY AMERCIAN DREAM!

In Ida's mind, her entrepreneurial plans always included her clan and vice versa. In the case of the Csiszars, family and business have intertwined all their lives; how they affected each other had always been in the forefront. Her entire life, Ida wanted to reach her professional goals because of and for her loved ones as they were top priority and sacred. While trying to achieve a great deal, she has always done her very best to be a warm and caring daughter, wife, mother, and grandmother—not just an average one. It was icing on the cake that she was able to create opportunities for her off-springs which only a few women of her era managed to accomplish.

The Csiszars has always been known for being positive. Even when someone passed away, they found a way to focus on the contribution of the deceased person as opposed to the loss and the sadness. While they were exceedingly work-oriented, they made sure that they took time off, relaxed, laughed, spent time with each other, and most importantly have loads of fun!

FULFILLING MY AMERCIAN DREAM!

Every year, after their big, multi-course, traditional holiday meal, they took a family photo. One year, like every year, the entire family lined up in front of the Christmas tree at "grandma's and tata's house," adults in the back, kids in the front, so the dedicated photographer could take a picture. When he was about to click the button, he noticed that Steve was missing. "He was just here a minute ago!" said one of them, "Where did he go?" said another. They were looking and yelling for him everywhere, but he was nowhere to be found when, suddenly, the grandkids spotted grandpa's feet sticking out of the branches at eye-level. Apparently, he had a bit too much fruit brandy and before the Kodak moment, he passed out backwards right into the Tannenbaum, miraculously still holding his glass upwards! That set the tone for the rest of the evening and ended up being one of the best Christmases ever.

Of course, that was not the only time they had tremendous amount of fun. At every celebration and on Sundays, Ida ordered an ice cream truck to drive straight to their house, serve the kiddos gelato.

This happened so many times that the children took the service for granted. For the longest time they thought this was something that happened in every household. As they were getting older, they realized that their grandparents had to work hard to make this happen for them and they became committed to continuing the family culture of work ethics way beyond being able to afford chocolate and vanilla.

The Csiszars they had an unwritten agreement: when they were not at work, they didn't discuss business. During dinners, at barbeques and birthday parties, they never talked shop. This simple rule kept everyone sane at home and level-headed at work, as one of them added.

Once on the job, they all took their responsibilities very seriously. Several of the grandchildren have worked for or are currently working at Classic or West Coast Cosmetics. From the very beginning, Ida backed them up one hundred percent and gave ther a chance to be part of the legacy to the extent they wanted to be.

FULFILLING MY AMERCIAN DREAM!

The grandkids' first beauty projects happened back in elementary school. When they had to complete a science project, one of them made soap and the other Chapstick. It certainly made it easier when you, as a child, had an entire factory at your disposal. The most important lesson Ida wanted to teach her grandsons was to believe in themselves; that it was possible to achieve whatever they set their hearts out to do. Her support went beyond verbal encouragement. As they were growing, she provided the boys with specific ideas, tools, and solutions in the areas of manufacturing, business, and marketing, in order to pursue their career goals.

Some of them stayed with one of their companies and some ventured out, but they all learned how much work and effort it took their grandparents and parents to build their facilities. This didn't come as a surprise. The family had strong entrepreneurial roots and the grandchildren grew up wanting to carry on their legacy. When they became adults and got married, their spouses too joined Classic Cosmetics making it an extended family enterprise!

FULFILLING MY AMERCIAN DREAM!

No Csiszar was purposefully raised or "groomed" for business, though. All of them learned by just watching the grownups being go-getters and ambitious. When Ida's son, Steven, first went to college, it was something he decided on his own because he saw the value in education. Not that his parents didn't want him to go to college, it's just that it wasn't the background they came from. Steven ended up being the first person in the family to get a college degree and once Ida saw the importance of it, she was on board with him going as high academically as he could. Later she advocated for the grandchildren to attend a university As a matter of fact she encouraged her employees to send their kids to college.

Now that Ida had been successfully making products for others for years, she wanted to expand. It was finally time to have her own makeup line. She called her brand Gallany which is a word that is made up: "Gal," her maiden name; and "lany" which means "girl" in Hungarian. She had dreamed of having her own product line ever since she worked at Max Factor; this was going to be her legacy. Now, in her mid 70s, she was ready to develop her repertoire of hues. Most new brands start with one color, Ida's product hit the market with 30 different lipsticks! The truth was, she could have stopped at the height of her career, but she was persistent and didn't want to retire without having her own passion product out there. In 2014, she launched her full makeup line, Gallany, manufactured by her company, Classic Cosmetics, and that made Ida exuberantly happy.

The brand had its unique marketing method which adjusted to the times. Online sales have changed retail considerably and it had definitely made an impact on cosmetics. Instead of reaching out to retail stores, they are online only as that's where the customers are these days. When you recognize a trend, you have to market immediately and accordingly. Gallany works with several Youtube-ers and bloggers; these are the ones who are driving the consumers to products. If a popular social media personality says he/she loves a given product, whether it's a boutique or mass market line, they instantaneously sell out. The social-media personalities are not celebrities in a classic sense, but companies like Gallany work with them to drive the market forward. Ida's makeup has been featured on multiple American channels and syndicated shows including Black Entertainment Television and the Wendy Williams Show.

Due to the fact that she started her own brand, Ida was invited to speak at many events. However, she never liked crowds, so she turned down the requests until one day she had to do an impromptu stage appearance at the Hungarian church to which she belonged. She got up on the podium and was crystal clear about going blank. She didn't know what to say, she was that nervous. Somehow, she ended up saying something, but she didn't recall what. All she remembered was that everyone was clapping, and people were coming up to her telling her how wonderful she was. Ida was glad they paid attention to her words because she certainly hadn't. While Ida went through many challenging moments in her life, none of them felt as horrifying as being in front of the public and she promised herself never to do it again and hurried back to Classic Cosmetics to focus on business growth.

FULFILLING MY AMERCIAN DREAM!

As Classic Cosmetics production increased, so did the factory's square footage and their number of employees. By 2018, they had 155 employees and about 150-200 long-term temps working in 110,000 square feet in three buildings that were 52,000, 28,000, 30,000 square feet. They owned 70% of the property that housed their facility, and Ida's factory grew bigger than Max Factor was at the time when she worked there.

Classic Cosmetics' minimum order in 2011 was 1,000-2,000 pieces for a single product in a single shade. During that time their average order was 5,000-10,000 pieces. The minimum order in 2016 was 3,000 pieces for a single product in a single shade and the only exception they made was for their long-term customers who had been with them for more than 15 years. Classic Cosmetics, being a loyal company, consistently accommodated their longstanding clients independently of their policies. In 2017, the average order was 100,000 but they had multiple 500,000-1,000,000 orders in a single shade for a single product. They also began to run second shifts with their machines that were automated, and results multiplied.

By 2015, Frank gradually grew into the role of the CEO of Classic Cosmetics while Ida now preferred being the chairperson. Today she no longer needs to be part of the day-to-day operation as much as she used to be, but she still has a good idea of what's going on. She goes to work four times a week and makes an effort to keep up with the times. At age 80, she has learned to compose an email, be active on Facebook, and make calls on Skype.

After so many years, industry professionals continue to seek out Ida and want to know in what she is currently involved. Her friends at other companies still send their employees to her if they need a solution and that makes her Ida feel appreciated.

Recently, she won a City Award for the Cosmetic Innovator of the Year for Classic Cosmetics Member's Choice Product which reall flattered her. No matter what her accomplishments she is still that humble, modest, and respectful person she was raised to be. Throughout the years, she has received several offers to sell the company, but it has never even occurred to her, as Classic Cosmetics is her legacy. Recently, the company added clients to its roster that are too famous to mention. Brands have become more secretive over the years and due to binding confidentiality agreements, the manufacturer can no longer share the list of their star clients. Know this though: if you have heard of the makeup brand, they are probably Classic Cosmetics' clients.

While running his mother's company, Frank also developed his separate enterprise, New Phaze. That being said, his main focus is Classic Cosmetics which he loves leading because he is being surrounded by incredibly effective department heads who are supportive of each other. Staff wise, he thinks, the company has the best people in the key positions as it has ever had.

Ida is much more relaxed now, because she sees that the team has everything under control, no matter how busy or hectic it gets. Frank is delighted that Ida is still with the corporation. If Frank has a challenge, he just walks over to his mother's office and asks for advice. He keeps Ida informed since she is still on the top of her game and mentally, she is laser sharp.

Ida is the first one to ensure that the company continues to do a lot for their staff. Frank too puts a lot of effort into keeping the family oriented culture strong so if any of them need help, they can get it either from the management or each other. It is not unusual for a worker to ask another to give them a ride or babysit their kids and later return the favor.

As it turns out adults too love ice cream trucks, therefore the company has one come in multiple times a year just to entertain their team. Since the grandsons were little, the selection of the toppings evolved quite a lot, so having gelato on the premises is even more of a treat than it used to be. The staff also receives a generous holiday bonus, as long as the company can afford it, and the amount is based on years of service with Classic Cosmetics. In addition, there is a huge holiday raffle to which the workers always look forward. Frank personally goes out and gets the impressive gifts and then the general manager herself wraps all of them for the banquet. The list of generosity doesn't stop there. If someone is hurting financially, they give employees an advance of up to $1000 and they offer an executive bonus program.

The overall welcoming atmosphere and the substantial benefits have resulted in her employees loving to come to work. A compounder once said that she looked forward to waking up in the morning and stepping on the premises, and on the weekends, she missed being there.

Ida's devotion to her staff created so much good for so many throughout the decades. She finds joy in offering her mentorship to others, sharing the recipes and secrets to makeup. Many feel that they received a first-class education they could not have gotten anywhere else. Ida genuinely revels in seeing others blossom; her people's happiness contributed to hers.

Even though she goes out of her way to make everyone's life better, some disappointed her by moving on right after they got what they needed. Ida got hurt when she heard that former mentees became her competitors when they started their own companies and they attempted to get the same customers Classic Cosmetics already had.

When Ida started her enterprise in Chatsworth it was the only business of its kind. Due to the governor getting rid of the requirements for cosmetics registration and FDA qualification were no longer needed, Ida's and Steven's former chemists had a much easier time establishing three of the five manufacturing facilities in the region and so the city has become a mini cosmetics Mecca.

FULFILLING MY AMERCIAN DREAM!

Even though their employees had to sign non-disclosure agreements, it was very difficult to protect the formulas. These days, any technician is capable of snapping a photo with their cell phone and that is all it takes to steal the patented blends. Some of the former workers took proprietary information with them and while it was unethical, going after them would have been difficult. Proving the theft would cost astronomical amounts and the compensation would not be significant enough. Also, while descriptions are important, they are not the key to success. Even if a recipe is unknown, a specialist or a compounder could figure it out eventually. That being said, it's not really worth spending time on it because launching something that is similar to a product that a big brand already has on the market, is of no interest to anyone and a big corporation would squash any individual in a legal suit anyway.

If one wants to find a formula, all one has to do is locate it online, in trade publications, and even vendors of raw materials provide them without hesitation. Unless the blueprint is for curing cancer, it no longer has real value. After all, the methodology, how something is made, has far more significance, and is worth a lot more.

After her initial disappointment, taking all this in consideration and with all fairness, Ida understood that her chemists too had their dreams on their own. She herself didn't stay with everyone who helped her along the way and neither did her experts.

Frank's vision for Classic Cosmetics is to go beyond producing make up only and upgrade to "do everything." Since they have their own machine shop, they are able to install a punch-press are that would make the pans that the powder goes into.

While leading the enterprises, Frank also enjoys life more than ever before. He still rides his chopper, not just his old Harley, but all of the vehicles from his significant collection of motorcycles, race boats, and sport cars. His love for them originated from his teenage years. He and Steve used to ride their dirt bikes, and today all of their sons have one too. Apparently, it's a passion of the Csiszar men and they refuse to quit.

There is one Csiszar though who no longer can say yes to riding. After a long illness Ida's husband, Steve, passed away leaving a big void in her, her children, and the grandchildren. Not just Steve himself, but their union was an inspiration to many. After a lifetime of caring for and taking care of each other deeply, she misses coming home to his cheerful lightheartedness. The example of their five and half decade long togetherness was not something her grandchildren's generation frequently sees. In fact, due to the high rate of divorce in society, her grandsons don't know any other real-life couple who had such a long-standing marriage. Ida's and Steve's dynamic sweetness is something these young men decided to strive for in their own relationships. To commemorate and celebrate their love, a few years before Steve passed away, they organized a 50th anniversary party for the couple with an incredible slideshow, and there wasn't a dry eye in the room. They learned that working hard and sticking to it doesn't only have significance in business but their personal lives as well. Knowing that their grandparents had to go through extremes and still found a common ground sent a message that will last for a lifetime. Ida also wished to show them the importance of keeping their focus on their goals. If one idea didn't work, one could try a different way. She believes that one has to take every opportunity because one never knows when that next big moment will arrive. If Ida had given up the first time, she surely would have lost out on several other ones.

After a lifetime union with Steve, after his passing, Ida found herself feeling lonely and alone and it didn't help that the company staff also seemed collectively sad. There was no longer this charming man passing around joy every day. It took a while for her to regain her strength but at the end she is a trooper and she didn't let herself go. Instead, she stayed strong, kept moving forward with her plans, and showed up to work even when she had a cold or a doctor's appointment. She was committed to continuing on and keeping her engine pumping.

FULFILLING MY AMERCIAN DREAM!

Focusing on the next generation is what keeps her motivated and leaving a legacy behind is extremely important to Ida businesswise as well as personally. Her grandchildren are extremely proud of Ida and her success and all they want to do is to catch up to her. Even though they are now grown, they still turn to her. Whether it's for equipment, marketing connections, or simple inspiration, when they go to her, Ida's gears start turning to find the right tools to provide. Ida is very accepting of her grandsons. They never feel judged whether they just got big tattoos or decided to go with an unusual career path. Ida created such a family culture that she is not the only one whom they can approach, but they also get support from each other. When they do seek her help, the beauty in their asking is that it does not have to be a request, just a statement of needing help and they receive it instantly since in their family that is a given.

Her grounded, savvy, and modest grandsons have let their passion be defined by Ida's example. They are building their lives and careers: Danny is a personal trainer, Cory is the Vice President of

Classic Cosmetics, Austin is a scientist, Devin is the Operations Manager and Shane is the General Manager of West Coast Cosmetics.

Some of them chose a career with Classic Cosmetics, but they have to earn their keep. They are treated fairly and there is no favoritism. Just like Ida, Steve, and Steven, the grandchildren have to take part in doing the dirty work. Ida doesn't let them take shortcuts because she wants them to learn from their own mistakes and roll with the punches.

Those grandchildren who chose a different career path and don't see her daily at work, stop by at her house at least once a week, and twice a month bring the great grandchild to see her.

CHAPTER EIGHT

Conclusion

The Realm of Rich Burgundy

As an immigrant, Ida built an empire and became the epitome of the American dream. She has done things a lot of people cannot even dream about, yet, she'll never act that way. Ida still lives in the medium-sized house with lots of plants that she shared with her husband for 23 years. She has aged gracefully, and her dresses are still stylish and always sophisticated. She didn't forget about those who aided her along the way: she frequently supports the Red Cross and the Salvation Army just as she said she would.

She loves to travel; she's been to Japan, Hawaii, Alaska, Italy, France, England, Romania, and Austria. She regularly visits Hungary and sometimes she goes together with Irene. Ida visited the Grand Canyon too and flew over it in a helicopter. Sixty years after she crossed the Atlantic Ocean from the Netherlands to Canada on the Holland American Line, she took a cruise to the

Caribbean at age 77. When she arrived at the harbor and identified which cruise liner, she had a ticket for, it read: Holland American Line. She didn't choose the ship then and she didn't choose it now, except this one was far bigger and even more luxurious.

Just like when she was younger, she enjoys being alone, yet her loved ones are more precious to her than they have ever been. She is now more open to life because she feels safe and protected. She frequently thinks about her life and how God picked her up, gave her opportunities, and showed her the way. All the good, bad, and the ugly ended up serving her. She is convinced that many doors got opened for her on purpose, yet she feels she is not special. For her entire life all she tried to do is to love what she did, push the rock up the hill, lead by example, and not accept failure. She credits God for her success; she says all it was "God guiding Gal."

After all these years, Ida still loves the Frank Sinatra song "You're Gonna Hear from Me" and frequently sings along with the lyrics when it comes on the radio:

FULFILLING MY AMERCIAN DREAM!

Move over, sun, and give me some sky

I got me some wings I'm eager to try

I may be unknown but wait till I've flown

You're gonna hear from me

Make me some room, you people up there

On top of the world, I'll meet you, I swear

I'm stakin' my claim, so remember my name

You're gonna hear from me

Fortune, smile on the road before me

I am fortune's child

Listen, world, you can't ignore me

I've got a song that longs to be played

Raise up my flag, begin my parade

Then watch the world over start comin' up Clover

That's how it's gonna be

FULFILLING MY
AMERCIAN DREAM!

I've got a song that longs to be played

Raise up my flag, begin my parade

Then watch the world over start comin' up Clover

That's how it's gonna be, watch me

You're gonna hear, you're gonna hear from me…

Made in the USA
Columbia, SC
23 March 2019